C000079870

Ragdale Hall

The Life and Times
of an
English Country House

Róisín Isaacs

First edition published 2001 by:

Ragdale Hall (1990) Ltd

Ragdale Hall, Ragdale

Nr Melton Mowbray,

Leicestershire LE14 3PB

Copyright © 2001 Ragdale Hall (1990) Ltd

All rights reserved.

No part of this book may be reproduced,
stored in a retrieval system, or transmitted in any form
or by any means, electronic or otherwise,
without permission in writing from the publishers.

Designed by Newham, Newark & Chambers Ltd. London.
Printed and bound in Great Britain by The Bath Press.

ISBN 0-9540946-0-3

Contents

Illustrations

Acknowledgements

No author of a history book can rely solely on their own resources for all the detail that makes a well rounded story. Therefore I am indebted to everyone who gave their time unselfishly to assist me in acquiring as much detail as possible through personal interviews. This list is enormous so I feel it is best for the reader, if I group the people who contributed to this book with some exceptions for personal mention.

The existing staff of Ragdale Hall, those who have worked at the Hall for over 20 years with their memories spanning several commercial ownerships and those who guided me to other sources in the community who had considerable knowledge of the Hall such as Neville Waplington.

The descendants of the Cantrell-Hubbersty family in particular Pippa Woodroffe, Philip Hales, and Jeremy Fordham for their in-depth detail of family characters and personalities, family photographs and memorabilia.

Local historian and Church Warden of All Saints Church, Ragdale Village, Tony Geary, who generously gave of his time to research, contribute and proof read the text.

The residents of Ragdale Village for their stories and memorabilia and the people of Melton Mowbray and surrounding districts for their many photographs, documents and newspaper cuttings generously lent to me for the benefit of the project.

The Melton Times Newspaper in helping to find contributors to the story and Melton Mowbray Library in assisting me with my research of history and character detail using their vast local history section and microfiche archive records of the Melton Times dating back to the late 19th century.

Finally, to everyone else connected with the story whose help and support has been invaluable. Nor can I impress upon you how valuable your contributions have been in making this story so varied and complete for the reader.

Preface

Whilst Ragdale Hall respects and understands the merits of both sides of the hunting debate, we would like to make it clear that the Hall is now in no way connected or involved in the hunting scene and has not been so for many years.

We would like to state that this historic story is not an attempt to write a hunting history book. The story of Ragdale Hall is an honest account of a country house built in 1785 as a hunting box for the local Shirley family. The Hall passed through many years of existence as a central location for those who wished to hunt in the Melton Mowbray area, until it became owned by a series of commercial enterprises who were not involved in the local hunting scene. The book focuses on the characters in the story throughout these times and their life interests as far as they are pertinent to the story.

The Directors of Ragdale Hall

Foreword

As the last living grandchild of Albert Cantrell-Hubbersty I was delighted to be asked to write a foreword to Róisín Isaacs' fascinating book on Ragdale Hall.

Albert's eldest son, Philip, was my mother's brother and therefore my Uncle. My earliest recollection of Uncle Philip is of a completely crooked man standing with his back to a blazing log fire. I always imagined him to be the man who stood by the crooked stile in my nursery rhyme book.

My Uncle Philip was known to be something of an eccentric and not one to be over expansive or subtle with his conversation. The last occasion I saw him was just after the war at my sister Birdie's wedding. He was asking my mother Augusta Margaret, known as Rita throughout her life, about the bridegrooms' prospects. I remember vividly the following conversation:

Philip: "Any money?"
Rita: "Enough."
Philip: "Parents alive?"
Rita: "No, they're both dead."
Philip: "No more to come then."

At this point he brought out an envelope and grunted "wedding present" and that was the end of that. The envelope contained a cheque for £5, not over generous even in 1946! (For the interest of the reader £5 in 1946 would be worth £115 today.)

I wish Ragdale Hall every success with this wonderful story and hope that many people will enjoy the book as much as my family and I will do.

The Old Hall, c 1750

Rakedale Old Hall,
Leicestershire. south front

Ragdale
the
Millennium
Village

Origins

Ragdale Village as viewed from Hoby Road

The village of Ragdale is first reported as an Anglo-Saxon settlement situated near the Roman Camp at Six Hills. During the reign of Edward the Confessor (c 1050 AD) the village consisted of six plough lands and was valued at 16 pence. Seric, a freeman "held 3 curacates at Ragdale". As expected, the village name of Ragdale has had a number of variations over its one thousand year existence. In previous times the village has been known as Ragendale (mentioned in the Domesday Book of 1086), Rakdale, Radgdale on the Willows, Rachedale, Rekedale, Rakedale, and more recently Wreakedale through to the early 1800's when the village became known by its modern name of Ragdale. The interpretation of the name can be "a settlement in a crooked valley" or a break or "rake" which forms a deep "dale". This deep dale starts about a quarter of a mile above the village and extends southwards for a mile, where it diminishes to allow a small brook to pass to Hoby and then into the River Wreake. The village is situated on the banks of this small brook or rivulet, which flows southward from the Wold Hills through this picturesque dale.

The 1086 records show that there were 20 people living in the settlement and the land, now under Norman rule, had been re-evaluated at 20 shillings. It was held by "Hugo under Robert De Buci". William the Conqueror later bestowed the land on his nephew, Hugh Lupus, Earl of Chester. Hugh Lupus gave it as a dowry, with his daughter Geva, to Geoffrey Ridell, from whom it passed through Maud, their daughter, to her husband Richard Basset, Justice of England, in the reign of the Norman King Stephen (1135-54).

The land subsequently passed to their son Ralph Basset whose chief seat was Drayton Basset in Staffordshire. Geva Ridell also gave All Saints' Church to the Priory of Canwell in Staffordshire during the reign of the Plantagenet King John - the patrons of the land and village from then on being the Bassets. King John is said to have often stayed in the vicinity of Ragdale and loved the area so much that he asked for his heart to be buried in Croxton Kerrial. This was executed according to his wishes and it is reported to lie there to this day. By 1220 AD the church had been taken into the Deanery of Goscote. In the Itinerary of 1280 AD "Rakedale, Wilghes, Radclive, Thrustington, and Houby" were all recorded collectively as one village. Later on, according to the Census of 1377, the population of Ragdale village alone had grown to 52 inhabitants.

The Shirleys

The Shirley family is believed to be of Saxon origin with an historic family seat at Ettington Park in the Valley of Stour, Warwickshire. In 1086 the Domesday Book, recorded that Sewallis held the manor of Ettington Park from Henry de Ferrers. It was a grandson of Sewallis who became the first "de Shirley" when he moved to the village of Shirley in the county of Derbyshire, while still retaining his interests in Ettington. In 1296 Warwickshire's first Member of Parliament in the reign of Richard II was Sir Ralph Shirley. To complicate historical matters many subsequent Shirley heirs were called Ralph.

In 1389 Ralph, Lord Basset of Drayton, holder of the manors of Rakedale and Willows, died without issue. He passed the lands to his nephew Sir Hugh Shirley of Staunton Harold, who also owned Breedon-on-the-Hill (Sir Hugh Shirley was the son of Lord Bassets' sister Isabella, and her husband Sir Thomas Shirley). However this transfer of ownership carried a difficult clause. Sir Hugh Shirley was obliged to adopt the name and arms of Basset. Hugh refused to change his name and arms, probably because those of the Shirley

The Old Hall,
c1750

family were more ancient and respectable, and so Hugh never officially came into the possession of the manor.

Sir Hugh Shirley was taken to court and sued by his cousin Edmund, Earl of Stafford and grandson of Lord Basset, who claimed that the lands should have gone to him as a result of Hugh's refusal to take the name of Basset. Sir Hugh did not live to see the dispute resolved as he died in the battle of Shrewsbury in 1409. Many years later Shakespeare was to commemorate Sir Hugh Shirley in the words of Prince Hal; "The spirits of valiant Shirley, Stafford, Blunt are in my arms now." (Henry IV part I, act V, scene IV). The dispute over the lands and names continued for 34 years until it was settled by King Henry VI in 1423, when the lands of "Rakedale, Willowes, Radcliffe, Barrow upon Soar, Dunton and Whatton" were handed over to Sir Ralph Shirley and his "lawfully begotten" male heirs. Ralph served under King Henry V in his war against the French and was at the siege of Harfleur in 1415. In 1423 the Shirley family established their family seat at Staunton Harold when the same Sir Ralph Shirley married Margaret de Staunton, who was heiress to her family estate. An original manor house existed at the time on the same site as the Palladian-style Hall that stands at Staunton Harold today. This more modern Hall was built by the 5th Earl Ferrers, Washington Shirley, in the 18th century.

Within the lands handed over to Sir Ralph Shirley in 1423, nestled a small local village called Wileges or Willowes, which existed until the middle of the 14th century when its sudden decline is explained away by two possible theories. The most probable is that it was due to the ravages of the "Black Death" but the second theory arises from a story that in 1495 the tiny hamlet had its thirty people turned away by Sir Ralph Shirley so that he could rear his sheep on the land. The story reports how the "people were turned away and they perished". The site of this hamlet can still be detected on aerial photographs of the area, its size being between 200-300 acres. This was not to be the last time that the Shirleys demolished a village. Many years later in 1795 they demolished another village in order to make way for enclosing their Ettington Parkland following a bill in parliament, which was promoted by Evelyn Shirley. Due to the acceptance of this bill Evelyn relocated a village to a new location two miles away at Upper Ettington. In 1509 another Sir Ralph Shirley leased the manor of Ettington Park to Mr. John Underhill while the Shirley's resided in Staunton Harold as their main residence. In 1541 the lease was renewed for 100 years at a rental of 40 marks per year. At this point the Shirleys had no immediate plans to return to Ettington Park.

In 1545 John Beaumont of Gracedieu, the representative of King Henry VIII in the dissolution of monasteries, obtained a licence from

The Shirley family crest

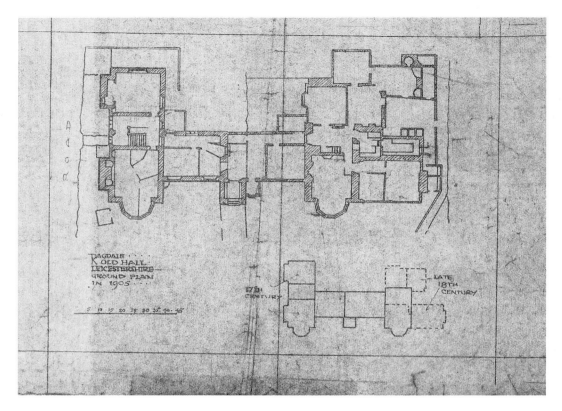

RAGDALE
OLD HALL
LEICESTERSHIRE
GROUND PLAN
IN 1905

5 10 15 20 25 30 35 40 45

17TH
CENTURY

LATE
18TH
CENTURY

Architects drawings the King to sell to Sir Francis Shirley of Staunton Harold, the rectory
of the Old Hall and vicarage of Rakedale. The property formerly belonged to the
room layout priory of Canwell in Staffordshire. The priory, which was dissolved by
and right Henry VIII, had been given, by Pope Clement VII, to Cardinal Wolsey
elevations for his founding of the colleges at Christ Church and Ipswich. Wolsey
in 1905 who had fallen out of favour with Henry VIII was detained for treason
and died in Leicester on his way to the Tower of London. Under the
ownership of the Shirley family, All Saints Church now belonged to the
manor of Rakedale and was included in the parish of Rakedale.

   The original Ragdale Hall in Ragdale Village, often referred to as
the "Old Hall", was located down in the dale of Ragdale beside the
existing church of All Saints', just one mile from the modern Ragdale
Hall that we know today. The Old Hall was built by Sir John Shirley in
the 16th century in the Elizabethan Period (1558-1603). Originally it
was built as a falconry lodge and was used for this purpose for many
years. The Old Hall was only ever occupied when a hunting party was
present otherwise it was largely closed up and used for keeping the
hunting hawks. During this time the Shirley main residence always
remained at Staunton Harold Manor.

   In 1611 George Shirley, a staunch Catholic, was elevated to the

SOUTH FRONT

Ragdale in 1905

ELEVATION TO ROAD

PART OF NORTH ELEVATION

peerage when he was created a Baronet by King James I. This reflects the importance of the Shirley family to the King at the time, as the family was elevated despite the king's staunch adherence to the Protestant Church and his determination to enforce its practices. Sir George's son, Sir Henry Shirley, was descended from the falconer of King Henry IV and as a soldier was once imprisoned in the famous Fleet Jail, London, due to a dispute over hawking rights. However he went on to acquire the Irish estates that remained in the Devereux family when he married Dorothy, the daughter of Robert Devereux, Earl of Essex. The estates had been acquired by her father, Queen Elizabeth's ill-fated favourite Earl, who had had a disastrous expedition to Ireland in 1599. It was from the Devereux connection the Shirley family adopted their family motto "Je Suis Loyal". Sir Henry greatly refurbished and embellished the Old Ragdale Hall in 1629.

Sir Henry Shirley had a great taste for heraldry and his own arms, set into the fireplace of the Old Ragdale Hall, had 52 quarterings and was dated 1631 with the initials H.D.S. for Henry and Dorothy Shirley. He set up a second coat of arms for his mother and another for his wife. This beautifully carved wooden fireplace, complete with coat of arms and initials as set out by Sir Henry can still be seen today in the

Newark Houses Museum in Leicester. In 1632 Sir Henry commissioned a very detailed family tree of the Shirleys, on parchment, which is now kept at Staunton Harold.

Sir Henry's eldest son, Charles, died in 1646 and his younger brother Robert, succeeded him. Sir Robert Shirley was intensely loyal to the lost cause of King Charles I and a defiant Royalist during the English civil war. Even after the defeat and execution of the King his loyalty to the Stuarts was unwavering. He succeeded to 4th Baronet at the end of the civil war in 1646. In 1653 as a mark of his defiance, he built a beautiful church in the grounds of the family seat at Staunton Harold. Cromwell was enraged at this act of defiance and held Sir Robert Shirley under suspicion of plotting to restore the Monarchy. Cromwell felt that if Sir Robert could furnish money to build a church, he could also provide funds to build a ship of war or raise a regiment. So, to establish Sir Robert's loyalties, Cromwell requested that Sir Robert furnish him with monies to support a regiment. Robert refused this request and as a result Cromwell had him arrested and imprisoned in the Tower of London where he died in 1656 at the age of 28 years, possibly the victim of poisoning.

The old Ragdale Hall was reputed to be one of the finest of its kind in the whole country. It was later extended by the next Sir Robert Shirley. This Robert was a grandson of Sir Henry Shirley and had an illustrious career, being made a Peer in 1677 and 1st Earl Ferrers in 1711. Robert frequently resided in the Hall while hunting and kept his hawks in their own room - the stone trough from which they were fed still remained in the Hall until the end of the 19th century. To put things in perspective, a hawk was of enormous value at that time and could be equal to the value of a whole village. Hence hawks were very well cared for by their aristocratic owners. Robert used the old Ragdale Hall solely when hawking. Sir Seymour Shirley, eldest son of Sir Robert, died in 1667 and was succeeded by his posthumous son Robert, who also died two years later. The baronetcy therefore passed to another Robert, second son of the cavalier. This Robert was a noted courtier who in 1677 was created Lord Ferrers of Chartley and, in the reign of Queen Anne, Viscount Tamworth and Earl Ferrers. The fecundity of this Shirley has earned him a place in the Guinness Book of Records. He had seventeen children by his first wife, ten children by his second, and in addition he fathered thirty illegitimate children - making a total of fifty-seven offspring! Upon Robert's death in 1717 the Warwickshire estate passed to the youthful eldest son of his second marriage, the Honourable George Shirley. George carried out much refurbishment of Ettington park and largely severed his

connections with the Leicestershire based Staunton Harold branch of the family.

The New Ragdale Hall in 1785

The Shirley's were generally known to be an honest and respectable family, but unfortunately the 4th Earl Ferrers, Laurence Shirley, clouded the family name in 1760 by murdering his manservant in a frenzy. He was tried by his peers in Westminster Hall and as a result was the last peer to be executed at Tyburn. Reported to be a fascinating personality, he is said to have had "graceful charm, erudition, and a waywardness, which led to the final damning incident in his life". Laurence went to the gallows in style. On the day of his execution he rode to the scaffold in a carriage drawn by six white horses and attended by liveried postillions. The last aristocrat in England to be executed for a felony, he was hanged by a silken rope in deference to his rank.

In 1785 the "New Hall" was completed and from that year the Earls Ferrers never again used the old Ragdale Hall as their periodic hunting residence. The old Hall was converted into two semi-detached farmhouses and rented out by the Shirley family to local farmers and tradesmen who used it as their home for over 100 years. It passed into the hands of Caroline, Duchess De Sforza Cesarini in the early Victorian year of 1837, following the death of her grandfather the 7th Earl Ferrers. Caroline never lived at the Hall but continued to rent it out to local people. Consequently the Old Hall became gradually more and more neglected.

Records reveal that in 1846 William and Henry Henton (gentleman farmers and graziers) lived at the Old Hall along with John Pym (joiner) and John Beeby and Samuel Hart (farmers). In 1863 Thomas Henton and John Nuttall (farmers) lived at the Old Hall. The Henton family was rather notable in the area. They were part of the local hunting set and often hunted with members of the Royal Family. As they were gentlemen farmers, they were heavily involved in the local community and today their gravestones may still be seen inside All Saints Church and in the graveyard in Ragdale Village.

The Parish of Ragdale

The Parish of Ragdale, bordered by the Fosse and Saltway ancient Roman routes, is in the Melton Mowbray Union and County Court District and East Goscote Hundred. Records of 1831 show that Ragdale was a village and parish, situated 12 miles north east of Leicester, 6 miles west of Melton Mowbray and 2 miles north of Brooksby station, containing 121 inhabitants and 1,421 acres of land. The living was a perpetual curacy, valued at 40 pounds and in the patronage of the Duchess De Sforza Cesarini, with the Revd. Edward Morgan, M.A., of Syston, as the incumbent. The church was dedicated to All Saints' and services were held at 10:30 am and 2:30 p.m., alternately with the church at Six Hills. The village has never had a large population. Even at its peak in the first half of the last century, when most rural areas were reflecting more interest in the land, records show that the village could only achieve 121 inhabitants.

In 1846 the parish contained 121 inhabitants and 1,421 acres of land. It included the ancient estate called Willoughes and extended westward to the Fosse-way, near Six Hills, one of the highest parts of the Wolds. By 1863 very little had changed in the village - the inhabitants were reduced by 1 to 120 in total and the acreage remained the same at 1,421. The living was still a perpetual curacy, valued at only 40 pounds and the incumbent was still the Revd. Edward Morgan. An infant school built by the Duchess De Sforza Cesarini opened in 1855. This was financially supported by local subscription but the schoolmistress Julia Lewin was paid by the Duchess. In 1871 the parish had grown somewhat to 127 inhabitants in 23 houses, and comprised 1,980 acres. The church curacy was held by the Revd. George Nesse Clark, B.A., who was by then also acting as incumbent for Saxelby with a benefice valued at 50 pounds. The village had become more established and the infant school mistress was Miss Ellen Henton.

This Anglo-Saxon village, which grew from a humble beginning, was to become the main support to a very large manorial Hall which was built in its midst. The existence of the great Hall, playing a hugely supportive role in this small community of people, undoubtedly helped to sustain it as a village to modern times. The Old Hall was finally demolished in 1956 amidst great objection from many members of the local community, who appreciated the value of restoring this great and noble edifice to something of its former glory and saving many of its treasures from destruction.

Caroline, Duchess De Sforza Cesarini

Descended from the Earls Ferrers and heiress to the Manors of Ragdale, Ratcliffe, and surrounding lands, Caroline, Duchess de Sforza Cesarini, was a very beautiful woman and, as such, was popular throughout all Europe. However, unlike many fine ladies of her time, the former Miss Caroline Shirley had a most uncertain beginning. Her father was Robert, Viscount Tamworth, the son of the 7th Earl Ferrers. Her mother was a servant girl who worked in the Earl Ferrers mansion. Robert fell in love with the servant girl but could not marry her and, as a result, Caroline was born illegitimately in about 1821. Robert died in 1824 while Caroline was still very young and, when the child was five years old, her mother, now the wife of a Syston landlord, was desperate to have her child grow up within the noble family from whom she was descended. Throwing herself on the mercy of the child's grandfather, the 7th Earl Ferrers, the former servant girl informed him that her child was the illegitimate daughter of his deceased son.

The old Earl was an irascible character who lived the life of a recluse - until this little girl came into his home. His Lordship was bewitched by his little granddaughter's beauty and her resemblance to his son Robert, from whom he had been estranged for several years prior to his death. The Earl adopted the child as his granddaughter and from that day on she was his constant companion. When he died Caroline was entrusted to the care of his great friend Charles Mundy of Burton Hall where she lived until she came of age. In 1830, while still only very young, she had already become Lady of the Manors of Ragdale and Ratcliffe, complete with the estate of 1400 acres.

Some years later a decently dressed woman, who was obviously not

The stained glass windows which Caroline installed in All Saints Church in 1874

of high birth, arrived at Burton Hall and demanded to see the young Lady Caroline. At first she was refused, but when she exclaimed, "Force only will remove me from this spot." the lady of the house was informed and she was struck by the woman's firmness. Eventually the visitor, who was Caroline's mother, was allowed to walk around the room in which her daughter was sitting at her drawing, with the express proviso that she should not address Caroline, or in any way allow the child to know her identity. This was agreed and the mother was taken around the room under the pretext of showing her some of the paintings and furniture in the room. Many years had passed since she had been separated from her daughter and Caroline had grown into a beautiful girl. The maternal feelings however, were still very strong. Pictures and furniture were unnoticed and the mother had eyes only for her daughter. Eventually her feelings overwhelmed her

and she fled from the room, never to see her daughter again.

Caroline was to go on to marry one of the most accomplished and aristocratic men in Europe, the Duke de Sforza Cesarini, related to the Dukes of Milan and descendant of the famous Medici family. Like Caroline he also had an unusual start in life. Before his legitimate birth, his parents had already settled their estates on a daughter born prior to their marriage. When their son arrived, after their marriage,

*The Old Hall
as seen from
the village*

they sent him to a foundling hospital where he was brought up before becoming apprenticed to a painter. Only two years before he met and fell in love with Caroline did he learn of his true identity and have his inheritance restored to him. Caroline married her Duke and settled in Italy. The Duke and Duchess de Sforza Cesarini, who resided in Genzano near Rome, came back to Ragdale Village incognito to paint the Old Hall. They travelled every day from Leicester to Ragdale for a fortnight and it was only when they were finally leaving and they gave a large donation for the peasantry, that their identity was discovered. "The little bells of the church of All Saints' soon proclaimed in their most gladsome notes, God bless our Landlord and Landlady the Duke and Duchess".

Caroline never forgot her people in Ragdale Village. She went on to build the village school in 1855, paying for the services of the schoolmistress. In 1874 she restored All Saints' Church, in her family's honour, complete with the beautiful stained glass window installed in memory of her ancestors. She continued to pay the village clergyman, whilst giving the sum of £5.00 (equivalent to around £195.00 today) to the poor each Christmas. Caroline had a daughter called Donna Vittoria who went on to inherit the Ragdale Halls and their estate lands upon her death at around the turn of the century.

The New Ragdale Hall

The "New Ragdale Hall" was built in 1785, in the Late Georgian period by the 6th Earl Ferrers. Built in the neoclassical style, again originally as a hunting lodge, it was a large, cemented building, considered modern for its time. It was situated on an elevated position north of the village of Ragdale, and was surrounded by an ornamental water-filled moat. It is described by Nicholls' History of Leicestershire as "the modern house" and is said to command "a delightful prospect" over the surrounding countryside, especially to the south where "the country in front forms an extensive valley, the Wreke running through it, whence gradually rising into hills, it has the appearance of a grand amphitheatre, seated on which are Burrow Hill, Billesdon Coplow, Tilton-on-the-Hill, Quenby Hall, and Gaddesby Church as principal objects". The text goes on to state "Melton Mowbray on the left, backed by Stapleford Hall, with several intervening churches, have a good effect". This elevated position affords the house incredible views of the surrounding countryside. On a clear day, one can see enormous distances. "It is supposed the extent of the view from East to West is upwards of 30 miles" (History and Antiquities of Leicestershire).

The New Ragdale Hall was also built for hunting purposes but by then foxhunting had taken the place of falconry. Although owned by the Earls Ferrers the New Hall was occupied on a rental basis by a number of gentlemen residents throughout the 1800's. In 1831 Hilton Jolliffe resided at the New Hall, then in 1846 William Richards (Gent) occupied the Hall until in 1880 when Mr Herbert Flowers took up residence. The Honourable Mr Pennington was the last occupier on a rental basis from 1885 until circa 1908 when it was finally purchased from the Earl Ferrers Estate by Albert Cantrell-Hubbersty in 1908.

The Honourable Mr. Alan Pennington

The most notable of these gentlemen residents was The Honourable Mr. Alan Pennington, who occupied the Hall from about 1885 until the late 1890s. J.O. Paget writes in his book, Memories of the Shires, "Mr. Pennington emigrated from Yorkshire, when, after trying South Leicestershire and the fringe of the Cottesmore, he eventually settled down in the Quorn country. Having married a sister of Captain Hartopp, he foreswore his Yorkshire birthright and became identified with the country of adoption".

Indeed he did become identified with his country of adoption. Alan Pennington was an avid foxhunter, who rode with the Quorn Hunt, playing an active role in the sport during the 1880s and 1890s. He was a fearless and excellent rider, often "leading the van" when, for example, fording a river or showing the following riders the way (Melton Mercury, March 1887). He had a quick, lively sense of humour and is described by Paget as the "genial humourist", always ready with a joke or a friendly taunt on old friends. Paget goes on to detail a foxhunting run which passes Ragdale Hall, "where the Penningtons then lived", dated Wednesday 13th March 1889. Just past Ragdale Hall there is an established Quorn covert called Schoby Scholes and this is where the hunt appears to have been heading on that day.

Alan Pennington was also a man of classical tastes as was displayed in his attendance at the Primrose League Concert at Melton in March, 1887, held on a Wednesday evening in the Corn Exchange at Melton Mowbray. The Melton Volunteer Band opened the concert and on that evening a series of male and female singers sang a variety of classical and semi-classical solos and duets. A comic song from a Mr. Oxley "greatly pleased the Gods" reported a much relieved newspaper reporter. The room was filled with a "highly respectable and appreciative audience" and in that appreciative audience, made up of the hunting society which included Dukes, Countesses, Majors and Masters, was a certain "Mr. Wilde who was also in attendance".

However, Alan Pennington also had a serious side to his nature.

Amongst others he was particularly irritated in 1886 by the suggestion that the farmers of the Quorn country should be consulted before a new Master of Foxhounds be appointed to the Quorn Hunt. He was further irritated when the farmers requested to be allowed representation on the Hunt Committee and, to promote this, they sent a list of names, suggesting those from whom representatives should be chosen. It was reported that, "Mr. Pennington did not see what right farmers had to see a hunt balance sheet".

Mr. Nuttall, the farmer leading the campaign, was inflamed by the inconsiderate attitude of the committee. He wrote a "fiery letter to the Leicester Advertiser" stating "he was calling another meeting of the farmers" and "as for rights, at least no hunt committee has the right to ride rough shod over us and insult us as well". However, matters settled down with the passage of time as it was reported, "subsequent proceedings were more amiable than anyone could have dared to hope". Interestingly one of the hunts great concerns, even in the 1880s, was that they avoid attracting undue attention by having an unnecessary "hunt row". Even then the opponents of foxhunting were often waiting in the wings for any dissention amongst the hunt committee. Anti-hunt opinions were held but it was not until many years later that these opinions were aired more fully.

Pennington was obviously a man held in high regard among the Quorn set of the time as he was the one chosen to be acting field Master, in the absence of the much admired Lord Hugh Lonsdale, for part of 1895. "Lord Lonsdale being at Lowther Castle, his

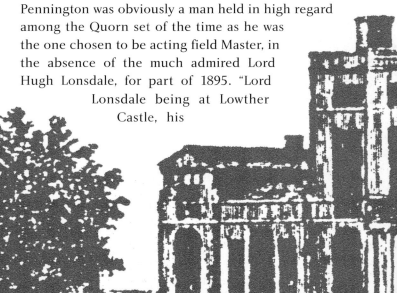

family seat, entertaining the Emperor of Germany". The private visit of Kaiser Wilhelm, a grandson of Queen Victoria, to his co-sailing friend Hugh Lonsdale at Lowther Castle, caused quite a stir in London and Berlin. The extent of Hugh's lavish entertainment, put on for the Emperor's visit, put something of a strain on his finances and a visit from the King of Italy shortly afterwards put further pressure on the Lonsdale coffers. Hugh's trustees quickly advised that he must cut his expenditure. So to comply with this request he decided to resign from the highly expensive Mastership of the Quorn at the end of 1896.

Lord Lonsdale was seen by the farmers as a good Master and a firm controller of the Quorn and his resignation came as a shock. So, on the 14th December 1896, just before moving off from a meet at Beeby, a Mr. Nuttall presented Lord Lonsdale with a petition to reconsider his resignation. "This was the same Thomas Nuttall of Beeby, who had lead the campaign of ten years earlier for the farmers to be represented on the hunt committee. Every farmer in the Quorn country had signed the petition" (Melton Mercury, 1896). Needless to say "Lord Lonsdale withdrew his resignation on the spot".

Although we are not informed what solution was found for the Lonsdale financial situation, it is worthy of note that, in hunting with the Quorn set, the Honourable Mr Alan Pennington, of Ragdale Hall in the 1880s, definitely rode with some rather elite and exclusive company.

Albert Cantrell-Hubbersty in the front garden at Ragdale Hall, 1912

The Cantrell-Hubbersty Half Century

1908-1958

Albert and Martha Cantrell Hubbersty

This most fashionable period in the history of Melton Mowbray commenced about the time of the purchase of Ragdale Hall by Albert Cantrell-Hubbersty. Albert was the youngest of three children, the son of Philip Hubbersty and Anne Augusta Hubbersty, of Wirksworth, Derbyshire. Albert's older brother William Philip, was born on May 30th 1840, his sister Frances Augusta on November 24th 1841, and Albert Cantrell on June 6th 1843. Originally from the Buxton area, the Hubbersty family's fortune had been built up, over a few generations leading up to Albert's time, from the ownerships of the Buxton Palace Hotel, the Buxton Lime Firms and The Buxton Stone Mining Company - at the time reported by the Melton Mercury to be "the greatest stone and lime concern in existence". Albert's mother was Anne Augusta, nee Cantrell, the only daughter and heir of William Cantrell of Alvaston Field in the Parish of Saint Michael, Derby, Master of Arts at Cambridge University.

Albert married Martha Lydia Jessop of Butterley Hall at Ripley in December 1876 when Martha was 17 years old, while Albert, at 33 years, was 16 years her senior. They had five children born between the years 1877 – 1891.

> **William Philip Cantrell Cantrell-Hubbersty,**
> known as Philip *1877 – 1947*
> **Augusta Margaret Cantrell-Hubbersty**
> known as Rita *1879 – 1968*
> **George Albert Jessop Cantrell-Hubbersty,**
> known as George *1880 – 1928*
> **Edward De Burg Cantrell-Hubbersty**
> known as Chang *1882 – 1960*
> **Mary Frances Cantrell-Hubbersty,**
> known as Midget or Midge *1891 – 1980*

Albert married as Albert Hubbersty but some years later changed his name through deed poll to Cantrell-Hubbersty in recognition of his mother's family name. This change was noted in a newspaper announcement on 9th February 1894. By this time Albert was already 51 years old. As per his wishes the family was officially notified that it could also bear the arms of the Cantrell family along side the arms of the Hubbersty family. This integration of names was confirmed on 10th April 1894, when Queen Victoria wrote to Albert at Felly Abbey, sending him the Royal licence, signed by the Queen, authorising the necessary name changes. This application had taken Albert some *feb: 9: 1894*

THE Queen has been pleased to grant unto ALBERT CANTRELL HUBBERSTY, of Felley Abbey, in the Union of Basford, in the County of Nottingham, Esquire, late Major and Honorary Lieutenant-Colonel 3rd Battalion Derbyshire Regiment, Lieutenant-Colonel Commanding and Honorary Colonel (1892) 1st Battalion Nottinghamshire (Robin Hood) Rifle Volunteers, in the Commission of the Peace for the Counties of Derby and Nottingham, her Royal License and Authority that he and his issue may TAKE and henceforth USE the SURNAME of CANTRELL, in addition to and before that of Hubbersty, and that he and they may BEAR the ARMS of Cantrell quarterly with their own family Arms, such Arms being first exemplified according to the Laws of Arms, and recorded in the College of Arms, otherwise the said Royal License and permission to be void and of none effect, and to command that the said Royal concession and declaration be recorded in her Majesty's said College of Arms.

HERALDS COLLEGE,
LONDON. E.C.
10 April 94

I send you herewith the Royal Licence signed by Her Majesty, authorising your change of name, which please acknowledge.

I am daily expecting to be able to send you the Boultbee report.

Yours truly

H. Farnham Burke
Somerset

To
Colonel
A. C. Cantrell-Hubbersty

years to complete but his determination was finally rewarded.

Albert moved homes frequently for his time. Before Ragdale Hall, the Hubbersty family lived firstly at Felley Abbey, "in the union of Barford in the county of Nottingham" and then at Tollerton Hall in Nottinghamshire. Albert and Martha were still living at Felley Abbey when their last child, Mary Frances was born on September 24th 1891. They then moved to Tollerton Hall sometime after April 1894.

Albert Cantrell-Hubbersty was a great foxhunting man, hunting in the early days with the Earl of Harringtons' hounds, formerly the South Notts Hunt. Albert and Martha would hunt up to six days per

Above, newspaper announcement of Albert's name change and right, letter from the Herald's College on the subject

Victoria by the Grace of God of the Un[ited] *Kingdom of Great Britain and Ireland Queen. Defender of the Faith. &c.* To Our Trusty and well beloved *Albert Cantrell Hubbersty, Esquire,* Gree[ting] We, reposing especial Trust and Confidence in your Loyalty, Courage and good Conduct do by [these] Presents Constitute and Appoint you to be an Officer in Our *Volunteer* Forces the *twenty-fifth* day of *June* 1892. You are therefore carefully and diligen[tly to] discharge your Duty as such in the Rank of *Lieutenant Colonel* in such higher Ran[k as] We may from time to time hereafter be pleased to promote or appoint you to, of which a notifica[tion] will be made in the London Gazette, and you are at all times to exercise and well discipl[ine in] Arms both the inferior Officers and Men serving under you and use your best endeav[ours] to keep them in good Order and Discipline. And We do hereby Command them to Obey [you] as their superior Officer, and you to observe and follow such Orders and Directions as from [time] to time you shall receive from Us or any your superior Officer according to the Rules a[nd] Discipline of War in pursuance of the Trust hereby reposed in you. Given at Our Court, at Saint James's the *eighteenth* day of *June* 1892 in the *fifty-fifth* Year of Our Reign.

By Her Majesty's Comm[and]

H. Campbell-Ban[nerman]

Albert Cantrell Hubbersty, Esquire,

Lieutenant - Colonel,

Volunteer Forces

The order from
Queen Victoria
regarding Albert's
appointment to
Lieutenant Colonel

week, but he was a military man and when Queen Victoria needed to ready her troops around the country he would answer the call to arms.

Queen Victoria notified Albert Cantrell Hubbersty on the 25th April 1892 that he was appointed as Officer in the Volunteer Forces from that date, commencing at the rank of Lieutenant Colonel. At this stage he was already Lieutenant Colonel of the Third Battalion of the Derbyshire Regiment and Honorary Colonel of the First Battalion of the Nottinghamshire (Robin Hood) Rifle Volunteers. In those days large estate owners were the prime source of the provision of men. Armies were raised on the strength of the loyal support of the landed gentry, their estate workers, and their tenants. There is no record however to indicate that, following this readiness, Albert did go to war at this time. Albert and Martha were still living at Tollerton Hall in 1898 when their daughter, Augusta Margaret, was married from there on July 6th at the age of 19 years.

Ten years later the Cantrell-Hubbersty's bought Ragdale Hall but they did not move into the Hall immediately as they wished to update the outer façade of the Hall with crenellations and small towers, reflecting the fashion of the day. The renovation of the Hall is reported to have taken some time but exactly how long is not clear. Local skill was used in the refurbishment programme, such as Mr. Eric Cropper's grandfather from the village of Hoby, who was engaged in the building and remodelling of the Hall.

On the 1st May, 1908 Albert, aged 65 years, bought the Ragdale Estate from the Cesarini family. Conveyancing papers from the sale list His Excellency Don Lorenzo, Duke de Sforza Cesarini of the first part, Luigi Medici Marquis De Vascello of the second part, and Her Excellency Donna Vittoria, Duchess Sforza Cesarini of the third part as interested parties.

Albert and Martha never lived in the old Ragdale Hall, which came into their possession purely as part of the estate. Records show that the whole estate was just less than 3000 acres at the time of this sale. The Old Hall remained as before, affording a semi-detached tenanted residence to two farming families. Like Alan Pennington before them, the Cantrell-Hubberstys lived their lives at the new Ragdale Hall. The Hall, although smaller than that at Tollerton, provided a family seat exactly where they wanted to be located, in the best and most fashionable foxhunting country England had to offer. The Cantrell-Hubberstys had located themselves in the heart of the most prestigious Quorn Hunt Monday country. There is some indication that Albert Cantrell-Hubbersty and his family may have kept Tollerton Hall on as a family home for some time after buying the Ragdale Estate, probably due to the renovations at Ragdale Hall.

Albert was most meticulous about family detail and, as part of the works in 1908, he commissioned the College of Arms to create a Cantrell-Hubbersty/Jessop crest which was positioned over the front door of the Hall where it can still be seen today. The Latin Motto over the crest of Cantrell is 'Pectus Fidele et Apertum', meaning "A faithful and open mind" and the Latin Motto over the crest of Hubbersty is 'Propositi Tenax' meaning "Firm of Purpose". Looking at the crest the husband's family arms are on the left and his wife's on the right.

In 1909, Albert commissioned an enormous clock for his newly built tower complete with five chiming bells. The clock, a Westminster timepiece, with 2 copper dials measuring 6 feet across, finished in black and gold was manufactured by John Smith and Sons Derby, while the bells were manufactured by John Taylor and Co. of Loughborough all in 1909. The five bells made for Ragdale Hall ranged from the smallest at 137lbs to the largest at 1423lbs together making a staggering total bell weight of 2493lbs, requiring a very special building structure to support a weight of such enormous proportions. Their details are listed by John Taylor and Co as follows;

No.1 bell – B weighing 137lbs measuring 1'6"
No.2 bell – A weighing 203lbs measuring 1'8"
No.3 bell – G weighing 249lbs measuring 1'10"
No.6 bell – D weighing 481lbs measuring 2'4"
No.10 bell – G weighing 1423lbs measuring 3'5" (the hour bell)

The hour bell with, inset, a detail of the inscription

The largest of these bells, the No. 10 bell, carries the inscription "One chime of bells, cast and erected by John Taylor and Co. Loughborough for Colonel A.C. Cantrell-Hubbersty Ragdale Hall, Leicestershire. 1909". This was an enormous undertaking for Albert but it clearly displays how affluent he was at this stage of his life.

Unfortunately in 1905, Martha Cantrell-Hubbersty then aged 46 years, suffered severe injuries when she was involved in a hunting accident while out with the Earl of Harrington's hounds, formerly the South Notts Hunt, in Nottinghamshire. She had followed these hounds for twenty years. Following this accident she was incapacitated for 5 years living at Ragdale Hall as an invalid. She finally died on June 18th 1910 aged 51 years old.

Hunting accidents were very much a part of the hunting society scene. The Cantrell-Hubbersty family was to have their fair share of such ill-fated luck over the generations. Albert, however died of natural causes on September 4th 1915, aged 72 years. The ownership of the Ragdale Hall Estate now passed to his eldest son and heir, Philip Cantrell-Hubbersty who was then 38 years of age.

William Philip Cantrell Cantrell-Hubbersty O.B.E., D.L.,

Known as Philip, he already had the reference to Cantrell in the last of his Christian names and as a result of his fathers' name change, Cantrell was again repeated in his surname. Two careers were becoming of the young highborn men of their day, one was the church and the other was the military. Philip Cantrell-Hubbersty was a military man.

Queen Victoria notified him that, from April 14th 1896, he was appointed to the rank of Second Lieutenant in the "Militia Forces". At this stage he was only 19 years old and the First World War was still 18 years in the future. He is referred to as a "Gent" on the notification.

His military career must have been quite successful because, on 1st of December 1897, Queen Victoria again notified him that he was Second Lieutenant to the "Land Forces". It is possible that he was playing a dual military role.

Philip Cantrell-Hubbersty, in the early 1940s

Later Philip was to play a vital role in the First World War, using his skills both as a soldier and as a fine horseman. During this war Ragdale Hall was used as a Re-Mount Depot for which Philip Cantrell-Hubbersty was mentioned in dispatches, only two months after his father's death in September, dated 30th November 1915. A re-mount depot was a store of horses which were broken in, trained, exercised, and readied for use in the war effort, both on home territory or, more urgently, overseas. The centre would also provide a service for horses returning from the war, where care or rehabilitation was required.

There is no information about Philip's actual activities at the war front, but he gained a second mention in dispatches for his time spent with the 15th Hussars, dated 8th November 1918.

The First World War resulted in extremely heavy casualties for all concerned and the experience put an end to cavalry being used again in warfare. Besides, enormous expenses were incurred whenever cavalry was deployed. Since all cavalry regiments were mechanised in the late '20s and early '30s, far fewer men and horses were lost to the ravages of the Second World War.

Victoria by the Grace of God of the United Kingdom of Great Britain and Ireland Queen, Defender of the Faith. &c. To Our Trusty and well beloved *William Philip Cantrell Cantrell-Hubbersty*, Gent. Greeting We, reposing especial Trust and Confidence in your Loyalty Courage and good Conduct do by these Presents Constitute and Appoint you to be an Officer in Our *Militia* Forces from the *fourteenth* day of *April* 1896 You are therefore carefully and diligently to discharge your Duty as such in the Rank of *2nd Lieutenant* or in such higher Rank as We may from time to time hereafter be pleased to promote or appoint you to of which a notification will be made in the *London Gazette*. and you are at all times to exercise and well discipline both the inferior Officers and Men serving under you and use your best endeavours to keep them in good Order and Discipline. And We do hereby Command them to Obey you as their superior Officer. and you to observe and follow such Orders and Directions as from time to time you shall receive from Us or any your superior Officer according to the Rules and Discipline of War in pursuance of the Trust hereby reposed in you. Given at Our Court at Saint James's the *thirteenth* day of *May* 1896 in the *fifty-ninth* Year of Our Reign.

By Her Majesty's Command

William Philip Cantrell Cantrell-Hubbersty, Gent.

2nd Lieutenant

Militia Forces

Communiqués sent by Queen Victoria to Philip in April 1896 and December 1897

Philip tried to sell Ragdale Hall together with its, now reduced 1,185 acres in September 1920. Unfortunately these large country piles were impossible to sell after the war and eventually removing it from the market Philip decided to continue using it as his family home. A few years later in the early 1920s Philip married Phyllis Bethell of Rise Park, Hull in Yorkshire. They honeymooned in Venice where Philip was unfortunately struck down with sunstroke on the third day of their holiday. Upon their return they decided to remain at Ragdale Hall and use it as their home. Phyllis, of a similar hunting family background was to make a very suitable wife. She understood his sentiments and his drivers even though she was not so involved in the hunting scene herself. She was to endear herself to the community at large and with her tremendous sense of humour, becoming a popular figure amongst her peers.

Philips' recognition continued to flourish between the wars and he was honoured when appointed Deputy Lieutenant of Leicestershire on the 23rd of August 1926. At this stage in his military career he had risen to the rank of Major and he was to be known as "The Major" by colleagues and friends alike for the rest of his life. In the mid '20s

Victoria by the Grace of God, of the United Kingdom of Great Britain and Ireland, Queen, Defender of the Faith, Empress of India, &c.

To Our Trusty and well beloved *William Philip Cantrell Cantrell-Hubbersty, Gent*, Greeting: We, reposing especial Trust and Confidence in your Loyalty, Courage, and good Conduct, do by these Presents Constitute and Appoint you to be an Officer in Our *Land* Forces from the *first* day of *December* 1897. You are therefore carefully and diligently to discharge your Duty as such in the Rank of *2nd Lieutenant* or in such higher Rank as We may from time to time hereafter be pleased to promote or appoint you to: of which a notification will be made in the London Gazette, and you are at all times to exercise and well discipline in Arms both the inferior Officers and Men serving under you and use your best endeavours to keep them in good Order and Discipline. And We do hereby Command them to Obey you as their superior Officer, and you to observe and follow such Orders and Directions as from time to time you shall receive from Us, or any your superior Officer, according to the Rules and Discipline of War: in pursuance of the Trust hereby reposed in you.

Given at Our Court, at Saint James's, the *twenty-fifth* day of *November* 1897, in the *sixty-first* Year of Our Reign.

By Her Majesty's Command.

William Philip Cantrell Cantrell-Hubbersty, Gent:

2nd Lieutenant

Land Forces.

Lansdowne

Philip was honoured with an O.B.E. in recognition of the services to his country, both as a civilian and a soldier.

Philip Cantrell-Hubbersty was a man of very few words. He would normally have conversation only with people who were involved in the foxhunting scene, and even then it would appear that his whole conversation would be along hunting matters. He was an avid hunter, usually riding to hounds six days a week. People who remember him say, "The Major lived in the saddle". Philip was a man who had little time for people generally, except those who did a consistently good job for him on his estate. He appreciated this type of person and he made time for them. Such as the blacksmith Mr Wall known as "Shoey Wall" who provided a mobile farrier service for the surrounding estates and the numerous stable yards in the area. Neville Waplington was another such person, helping Philip to remedy any large or small maintenance problems in or around the Hall and Estate. Neville "liked the Major"; he "got on quite well with him". It would seem that Philip held people in high regard if they had the kind of skills he needed for the job at hand and carried out their tasks to a high professional standard. Neville Waplington worked for many years for Garners in

1st mention
in Despatches

The War of 1914-1918.

Remount Service

T.(Maj.(Lt. R. of O.) W. P. C. Cantrell-Hubbersty.

was mentioned in a Despatch from

Field Marshal Sir John D. P. French, G.C.B, O.M, G.C.V.O, K.C.M.G

dated 30th November 1915

for gallant and distinguished services in the Field.
I have it in command from the King to record His Majesty's
high appreciation of the services rendered.

Winston S. Churchill

War Office
Whitehall, S.W.
1st March 1919.   *Secretary of State for War.*

Melton Mowbray. Garners provided a considerable building and maintenance service to the surrounding district, its large houses and estates, the hunting scene and its followers. This service included maintaining all the vehicles driven by these clients.

Unfortunately Major Cantrell-Hubbersty was simply not a good driver. During the Second World War years he had a black Ford Prefect. He would go to Melton Mowbray every Tuesday to meet all his friends at either the Bell or George Hotels. The Garner staff were not

2nd mention
in Despatches

L.G. 31077.   A/908.

The War of 1914-1918.

15th. Hussars.

Capt. [T. Maj.] W.P.C. Cantrell-Hubbersty, R. of O.

was mentioned in a Despatch from

Field Marshal Sir Douglas Haig, K.T. G.C.B, G.C.V.O. K.C.I.E.

dated the 8th November 1918

for gallant and distinguished services in the Field.
I have it in command from the King to record His Majesty's
high appreciation of the services rendered.

Winston S. Churchill

War Office
Whitehall, S.W.
1st March 1919.   *Secretary of State for War.*

allowed to go out on calls on Tuesday's, as they had to provide parking and valeting services for the many cars. "The Major" would pull up in front of the building and call out "Garner's man - park the car!" This was usually about 10.30am. At precisely 2.00pm the Garner's man had to bring the car back to the front door and have it turned in the direction of Ragdale Hall. "The Major", who would have had a few drinks over lunch, would now have to drive himself back to the Hall. He would get into the car, put his foot on the accelerator, put the car into top gear, nearly stall, and then GO! The car went up the road,

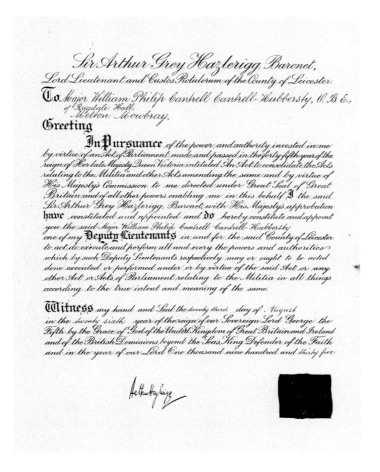

Above,
Sale document
September 22nd
1920 and left,
Communiqué
notifying
appointment of
Deputy Lieutenant
of Leicestershire

kangaroo style, in top gear, until it gathered some speed. It would appear, from the recollections of local people, that he never changed gear! Luckily for Philip, horses didn't have gears, or he would never have achieved his legendary status as the fastest man across the turf in Leicestershire in his late 60's. Apparently he was a fearless rider but somewhat single minded, as he would do the unforgivable and "take his own line" across the fields when riding behind the Master of the

Hunt – who at that time was Sir Harold Nutting. Although the two men were very good friends, Harold would be furious with Philip for this gross display of bad behaviour.

Philip was very territorial and competitive with his peers. Even though he was indebted to Garner's company for the supportive role they played in his lifestyle, he could not accept the fact that the company owner, Mr. Garner, came home from India after the war as a Colonel. This was not at all well received by Major Cantrell-Hubbersty and the old Major never accepted Garner as anything remotely close to an equal. As far as Philip Cantrell-Hubbersty was concerned the hunt was where the pecking order was established and he always made sure that Colonel Garner stayed well behind him in the hunting field. There was also a little rivalry between Major Cantrell-Hubbersty and Colonel Coleman of Scalford Hall in the Belvoir country. Colonel Coleman was of the Coleman's Mustard dynasty, but this didn't cut the mustard with Philip Cantrell-Hubbersty. Colonel Coleman was seen as a lesser individual and was treated as such any time their paths crossed in the hunting field. Needless to say Colonel Coleman and Colonel Garner were good friends and always supported each other.

Simon Blow in his book Fields Elysian speaks of Philip in a more domestic sense. It is said that Philip loved his wife Phyllis although it is uncertain if this affection was reciprocated. He was so focused on his own world and so limited in social graces that, when he and Phyllis were having a dinner party at the Hall, he would be rather restrained in his conversation during the evening and then, when he felt that he had had enough socialising, he would turn to Phyllis and say, "When are they going, Puppy?" ("Puppy" was the pet name they called each other through their time together as husband and wife.)

By the time of the Second World War, Philip was too old to be directly involved in the war itself but he played a key role for the Quorn Hunt. Wartime was always a struggle for foxhunting as the funds required to keep the hunt maintained were considerable. The hunt was financed by subscription and, as greater numbers of the younger hunt members went to war, subscriptions fell and the future finances looked bleak. Therefore, if the hunt did not have a benefactor at such times it could possibly collapse. The Quorn Hunt was then one of the greatest hunting packs in the country. It was inconceivable to Philip that the Quorn might suffer as a result of the war. Foxhunting had been badly pegged back throughout the country, as a result of the First World War. The experience had left its mark in the minds of the gentry and they were determined that, at all costs, hunting - "the sport of Kings"- must survive for future generations.

Philip could see that the Quorn Hunt was at risk and to prevent any deterioration in his key interest he decided to fund the Quorn himself throughout the war years. This he did at great expense. In the book Hunting in Paradise it is stated that, "the Quorn owed its war-time survival to a devoted foxhunting eccentric, Major Philip Cantrell-Hubbersty of Ragdale Hall". In 1933 he became Secretary to the Quorn and through the war years from 1940 he took on the position of acting Master of Foxhounds, which he continued until his death in 1947.

He financed, supported, organised, and operated the hunt, covering all its facets of need throughout this period. As Master he was well liked by the farmers over whose land the Quorn hunted. He treated farmers with respect and was always keen to visit them after the hunt had ridden over their land. He would help them check for any damaged fences that might need to be repaired, or help to solve any other problems occurring as a result of the hunt passing through.

After the war the young men started to return home, and Ulrica Murray-Smith told the story of Teddy Bouskell-Wade returning to the Quorn Hunt for the first time. Ulrica said, "Philip Cantrell-Hubbersty rode up and asked him where he had been and why he had not been out hunting. Teddy replied that he had been overseas fighting in the war". Philip was said to reply to the young man "Well, you will find that the subscriptions have gone up" after which he simply rode away! However, Philip's contribution to the Quorn Hunt through the lean years of the war was of immense importance to its survival.

The Quorn Hunt at Ragdale Hall in the 1930s with Philip on the far left. Also pictured are Sir Harold Nutting M.F.H. and Lady Nutting, George Barker and Lady Ravensdale

Philip, second right with George Barker, Mrs Cotton and Mrs Everard

On 22nd March 1947 Major Philip Cantrell-Hubbersty died as he had lived - out hunting with the Quorn. Like his mother and his brother before him Philip was killed as a result of a riding accident when, during a hunt on the Beacon Hill in Charnwood Forest, his horse caught its foreleg in a rabbit hole, threw him and then rolled on top of him. Local newspapers reported the accident, stating that he had died before the ambulance arrived from Loughborough. A quote about the accident from Mr. George Barker, the Quorn huntsman said "The meet on Saturday was on Rothley Plain, and there was little hunting in the morning so the horses were not exhausted. On Beacon Hill at about 3pm, a fox was sighted and the hunt broke into a canter. Major Cantrell-Hubbersty was about a hundred yards behind and was following a line through the bracken. A witness heard a shout and turned around to see the Major's horse standing riderless. He went back and saw the Major lying on his back. There was no apparent sign of life. The witness, Mr. Robert Spoor, went to him and put his arms around him. The Major looked up and said "My back…back, Bob" and fell back. A Doctor was sent for and arrived twenty minutes later. The Major's horse was well mannered and absolutely safe". Dr McOuat of Loughborough attended the scene on that fatal day. He reported that there "was no sign of any gross injury, but it was possible that the

Major might have sustained a fracture of the dorsal vertebrae. The Major had suffered from a condition of his arteries, inhibiting circulation and that kind of fall, with shock, might cause death without serious injuries".

Philip was no stranger to accidents in the hunting field. At the time of his death the local newspaper, the Melton Mercury, stated that he was attributed with "having been injured more times than any other rider, and though a cripple by the time of his death he continued to be a fearless rider". The paper goes on to report, "In November 1938 he met with a serious accident while hunting with the Quorn at Wymeswold. His horse fell at a stiff obstacle (probably a very high gate or hedge, as the Major was noted for attempting any such obstacle) and, rolling over him, caused a fractured pelvis. In the early part of 1926, he broke a leg while hunting with the Belvoir. In 1896, when acting as a judge of hunters at the Peterborough Show, a horse he was trying fell and rolled on him, dislocating a shoulder and fracturing two of his ribs". At the time of his fatal accident, Philip's wife, Phyllis, was in Italy and unable to return to England in time for his funeral. She sent a huge cross of red tulips as a wreath for the top of the Major's coffin. Philip was 69 years old when he died. He had previously told his friends of his expressed desire to die in the hunting field. The ownership of Ragdale Hall and Estate now passed to Phyllis.

Newspaper reports of Philip's accident and funeral

The funeral service was conducted at All Saints' Church, Ragdale by Philip's brother in law, Archdeacon J.P. Hales, assisted by the Revd. H. A. Beresford, Rector of Hoby. The Major's funeral attendance list reads like a page from the Who's Who of the hunting scene of the day, clearly showing a cross section, frozen in time, of the people who were involved in this sporting world at the end of its high period in the '40s. Several hundred people swelled the usually small number of Ragdale Village inhabitants in their attempt to pay their last respects to this very popular Quorn Hunt Master of Foxhounds. Many of the mourners had to stand outside the tiny church of All Saints', which

"ALL SAINTS," RAGDALE

✝

William Philip Cantrell
Cantrell-Hubbersty

OCTOBER 24th, 1877
MARCH 22nd, 1947

THE QUORN'S TRIBUTE

QUORN HUNTSMEN carrying the coffin of Major W. P. Cantrell-Hubbersty, who was killed in the hunting field at Beacon Hill on Saturday. The Major had been acting Master of the Quorn during the war years. The funeral took place at Ragdale Church.

Philip's funeral procession to All Saints Church and above, his funeral service booklet

Philip had owned and where he had requested to be buried. Although Mrs. Cantrell-Hubbersty was absent, many other members from both sides of the family attended this high society funeral. Philip's sister Augusta was present with her son, the Revd. George Hales. Also in attendance from the family were Mr. and Mrs. C.M. Fordham (nephew and niece); Mr. and Mrs. H. Markham (nephew and niece) and Mrs. L. Huskinson (niece). On his wife's side of the family the representatives were, Mr. A. Bethell, Mr. C. Bethell, Mrs. R. Blow (niece), Major and Mrs. Johnson of Boston, (cousins) and finally the executor of Philip's will, Mr. R Ford, another cousin, completed the family party.

Among close friends present on the day were the Countess of Lonsdale, Lord Hazlerigg, Lord and Lady Daresbury, Lord Allerton, Lord Newton-Butler, Captain Ronald Strutt, representing his father Lord Belper, Ronald's sister Lavinia, the Duchess of Norfolk, Lady Pilkington, Lady Nutting, Lady Helena Hilton-Green and Sir Edward Le Marchant. The Hunting fraternity was represented by Sir Henry Tate, Master of Foxhounds, Captain Maurice Kingscote of the Meynell Hunt, Major James Seeley of the South Notts Hunt, Mr. G. Tongue of the Belvoir Hunt, Major W. Pott, representing the Hunt Secretaries Association and Colonel H.K. Bruce representing old comrades of Philip's regiment the 15th (The Kings) Hussars. Many more people attended from the hunting membership including Mr. and Mrs. George Barker with their children Leslie and Esme. The reception which followed the funeral was held at Ragdale Hall. A small party of people peeled away from the reception to hold an emergency meeting in the Library on the future

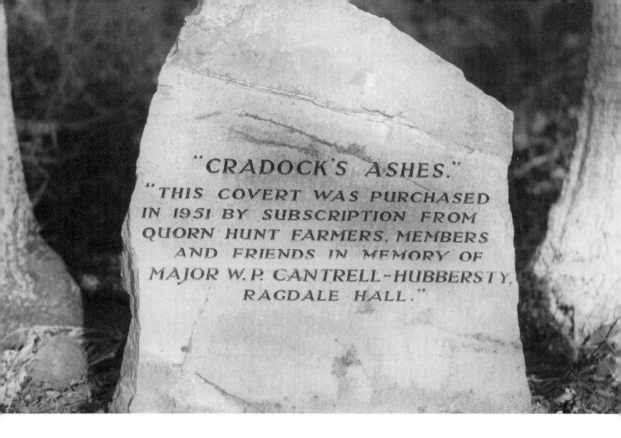

"CRADOCK'S ASHES."
"THIS COVERT WAS PURCHASED
IN 1951 BY SUBSCRIPTION FROM
QUORN HUNT FARMERS, MEMBERS
AND FRIENDS IN MEMORY OF
MAJOR W. P. CANTRELL-HUBBERSTY,
RAGDALE HALL."

of the hunt. The questions on everyone's lips were who would fund the hunt now that Philip was gone? Who was going to be the new master because with it came considerable responsibility and expense? This untimely meeting naturally upset the family who felt that the hunting

Above, "Cradock's Ashes" memorial stone and left, Philip's niece, Pippa, by his headstone with, inset, a detail of the inscription

Bequests to staff and Hunt servants

£93,000 WILL OF MAJOR CANTRELL-HUBBERSTY

BEQUESTS to Quorn Hunt servants and the staff at Ragdale Hall were left by the late Major W. P. Cantrell-Hubbersty, hon. secretary and acting-Master of the Quorn, whose estate is valued at £93,279, with net personalty £78,894.

He gave all his personal effects, live and dead farming stock to Mrs. Cantrell-Hubbersty absolutely, and bequeathed the following legacies payable on death: To his cousins, Violet Geraldine Ley and Nancy Farquhar £200 each; to his niece Mrs. Fordham £300.

HUNT AND STAFF LEGACIES

To the following, all of the Kennels, Barrow-on-Soar: George Barker (the huntsman) £125, William Grimmer £100, Leslie Barker £250, Esmé Barker £25, Jack Littleworth £50, Jack Smith £50, Fred Saunders £50, Cyril Jordan £25, and P. Hatcher £25.

The legacies to his own servants at Ragdale Hall included £100 each to Stanley Paulson, F. Ward, M. Scoley and Jean Todd, £50 each to W. Warnes and P. Boddy. To Fred Harris (secretary of the Hunt) £50.

His brother and sister, Mary Frances Cantrell-Hubbersty and Edward Cantrell-Hubbersty, received £100 each.

To the present joint-Master, Mr. Fred Mee, was bequeathed the choice of one of his horses as a token of friendship.

Subject to the payment of the above legacies the residue of the estate, including Ragdale Estate (but in this case at the discretion of the widow) was left upon trust for sale to his widow for life, and after her death subject to the payment of the following additional legacies: Leslie Barker £1,000, Esmé Barker £250, Philippa Ley (niece) £2,000, Joan Grimmer £200 and the ultimate residue to his niece, Mrs. Fordham, and his nephew, the G. F. Hales equally.

Above, details of Philip's will

folk were rather unfeeling and insensitive, but it does demonstrate the focus, that those involved in the hunt had on the vacant master situation. Some time later, after arriving back from Italy, Phyllis Cantrell-Hubbersty placed a sundial on her husband's grave as a head stone saying, with her usual high-spirited sense of humour, "You see, we will always be able to tell the time by him".

In 1951 the local farming community paid further homage to Major Cantrell-Hubbersty when they organised fund raising through collections and subscriptions and bought the famous coven "Cradock's Ashes". The coven was presented to the Quorn Hunt by the farmers and a memorial stone erected on the site in his honour.

Augusta Margaret Cantrell-Hubbersty

Born in 1879, Augusta, known throughout her life as Rita, was the first of two daughters. Augusta was always very close to her mother Martha who, having been married at the age of 17 years, was more like a sister to her than a mother. Like other young highborn ladies of this period, Augusta rode sidesaddle and hunted with the rest of the family, originally with the South Notts.

Augusta, had received a scanty education as the family emphasis was on hunting. They hunted on average six days a week, although, in order to fit in some education, Augusta only hunted three days a week. Augusta's education was compromised by sporadic attendance in the schoolroom and further compounded by a series of governesses who themselves had varying levels of educational skills. It is remembered that all the children had to learn to play the piano, which was unfortunate as not one of them appeared to have had an appreciation of tone or pitch.

Augusta was an affectionate girl and often found herself playing surrogate mother to her younger sister Mary Frances known as Midge, who, as the youngest of the children, was quite disliked by her mother. Sadly there seems to have been no love at all present for Midge as Augusta admitted to other members of the family that her mother Martha was really horrible towards the young girl. Augusta confided that her one concern on her wedding day was that she was going to be leaving her little 6 year-old sister and, of course, Augusta's marriage would have heralded a major loss to the child.

Augusta's wedding day, July 6th 1898, dawned bright and sunny. Before she left her family home of Tollerton Hall for the last time, a private photographer captured the moment, and her youthful beauty, for ever. The photograph on the opposite page displays the sumptuous detail of her late Victorian wedding dress, the quality of the internal

*Augusta on her
wedding morning,
July 6th, 1898*

soft furnishings to which Augusta was accustomed while growing up and the intricacy of the interior décor of a small portion of one of the

*Augusta's
wedding cake*

rooms at Tollerton Hall on that special day. Augusta's wedding cake, as seen above, also bore the similar intricate details characteristic of this late Victorian time.

Augusta had a sensible approach to life for, when an old Aunt asked her to choose her wedding gift from a Beckstein upright piano, a Brougham, which is a carriage or a piece of jewellery, she worked out her choice in the following way. She expected to inherit her mother's jewels, so she didn't need a gift of jewellery. If she had a carriage she would need a coachman to go with it so she wouldn't have that and, as she hoped to have a family, she would like all her children to learn to play the piano. She chose the piano. Augusta went on to become a wonderful mother of five children and the recipient of a portion of her brother George's will upon his untimely death in 1928.

George
Cantrell-Hubbersty

George Albert Jessop Cantrell-Hubbersty

George was a stunningly good looking man and very attractive to women. George really was the male star in the Cantrell-Hubbersty family. Unlike his brother Philip, George had the personality to go with it. He was very sociable and didn't live just for the hunting scene. He was a great friend to all the Birkins and of course knew Freda Dudley-Ward (nee Birkin) very well. Freda was a cousin to George's future wife Hilda St. Maur Willoughby. Like his elder brother, George had a successful military career.

On March 7th 1903, King Edward VII notified George that he was appointed 2nd Lieutenant in the "Yeomanry Forces". George was 25 years old and in the notification he is referred to as 'Gentleman'. By the time George was wounded in action in December 1917, his military

Edward by the Grace of God, of the United Kingdom of Great Britain and Ireland and of the British Dominions beyond the Seas, King, Defender of the Faith, Emperor of India, &c.

To Our Trusty and well beloved George Albert Jessop Cantrell-Hubbersty, Gentleman Greeting: We, reposing especial Trust and Confidence in your Loyalty, Courage and good Conduct, do by these Presents Constitute and Appoint you to be an Officer in Our Yeomanry Forces from the Seventh day of March 1903 You are therefore carefully and diligently to discharge your Duty as such in the Rank of 2nd Lieutenant or in such higher Rank as We may from time to time hereafter be pleased to promote or appoint you to, of which a notification will be made in the London Gazette, and you are at all times to exercise and well discipline in Arms both the inferior Officers and Men serving under you and use your best endeavours to keep them in good Order and Discipline. And We do hereby Command them to Obey you as their superior Officer, and you to observe and follow such Orders and Directions as from time to time you shall receive from Us, or any your superior Officer, according to the Rules and Discipline of War, in pursuance of the Trust hereby reposed in you.

Given at Our Court, at Saint James's, the Twenty-eighth day of February 1903 in the Third Year of Our Reign.

By His Majesty's Command.

St. John Brodrick

George Albert Jessop Cantrell-Hubbersty, Gent:

2nd Lieutenant

Yeomanry Forces.

career had progressed well. He was already a Major and was further honoured with a D.S.O. (Distinguished Service Order) towards the end of the First World War in early 1918.

As a person he was much loved by everyone and very popular, in particular with his young niece Margaret Hales who absolutely idolised him. Unfortunately however, he too could be beastly to his little sister Midge, if she got in his way.

When he married, George chose a bride from the very suitable family of Willoughby, with whom he had had a long acquaintance. His bride's parents were Harriet Maud Willoughby (nee Birkin) and Cecil Edward Willoughby. Cecil Willoughby was a Navy man, the son of the Honourable Charles Jeremy Willoughby and also nephew of Lord Middleton. It is worthy of note that Lord Middleton was also Phyllis Cantrell-Hubbersty's grandfather, thus making Hilda St. Maur Willoughby and Phyllis Cantrell-Hubbersty second cousins.

Hilda St. Maur Willoughby was born on the 16th September 1885 and met George through the mutual hunting field of the South Notts Hunt. The Cantrell-Hubbersty family had a long association with the South Notts and Hilda's cousin, Major Frank Seeley, was the Master of Foxhounds for the South Notts during the '20s. Hilda and George married on the 9th July 1913. Interestingly, Hilda's cousin, the society

George on horseback serving with The South Notts Regiment

beauty, Freda Birkin chose the same day to wed her first husband William Dudley-Ward. However George and Hilda's marriage survived for only nine years, ending in divorce without issue in 1922. Hilda remarried again in the same year to George's best friend Brigadier General Rupert Farquar-Riley. They went on to have a son Nigel Farquar-Riley.

Unfortunately George only lived for 6 years after his divorce from Hilda, as he suffered a serious riding accident on February 11th 1928, when, aged 50 years, he was returning from the hunting field and died as a result of a fall from his horse. It is believed that George's temper may have played a part in his demise because it is thought he was

In loving memory of
Colonel Albert Cantrell
Cantrell-Hubbersty, V.D.
of Ragdale Hall.
Died September 4th 1915.
And of his wife
Martha Lydia,
Died June 16th 1910.

Pippa by the graves of George and his parents, All Saints Church, Ragdale Village

killed when riding home recklessly to Carcholston Hall near Bingham, following a row with one of his fellow hunting colleagues. He was secretary to the South Notts Hunt at the time of the accident. On hearing the news of the accident, Edward Prince of Wales (a personal friend of George's), called Midge and told her that he was sending his own physician to attend George at Carcholston Hall. George lived for a couple of days after the accident but died just as the Prince's physician arrived at the Hall. Like his parents before him, George was buried in the graveyard of All Saints Church, Ragdale.

When Hilda St. Maur Willoughby married George, she brought another sport into the Cantrell-Hubbersty set, as the Birkin family was highly represented in the car racing scene. Hilda's mother was a Birkin, Freda Dudley Ward (nee Birkin) was her cousin and the famous racing driver Tim Birkin or, as he was officially known, Sir Henry Birkin, was also her cousin. Tim, known as one of "The Bentley Boys", was an avid car racing enthusiast, spending most of his time and money on the sport. He inherited 3 million pounds in 1928 (equivalent to 84 million today) on the death of his father and five years later he had spent it all on car racing before his untimely death from septicaemia, following a burn to his arm, in 1933. In 1932 Tim wrote a book called "Full Throttle", which is a riveting account of car racing in the early part of this century, clearly highlighting England's absolute reluctance to get involved in the European car racing scene of the time.

Tim was a great friend of the 6th Earl Howe, Edward Richard Assheton Penn, C.B.E., who was also a keen racing driver. Earl Howe was President of the British Automobile Association Racing Club and Institute of Road Safety Officers based at Brooklands. Tim won Le Mans with Earl Howe in 1928, and Earl Howe honoured Tim by writing a foreword for him in his book. In the foreword Tim is described as a "brilliant sportsman" and "a driver who is at his best on the road". This was, presumably, in comparison to a driver who was good on the track, although Tim was obviously very accomplished on the track as well, as Earl Howe goes on to say, "he has completed over 50 laps at 135 m.p.h. or more and now holds the Brooklands Lap Record of 137.89 m.p.h." This was achieved in Tim's single seater Bentley. Tim Birkin remains one of the country's unsung heroes – a motivating force in the British racing car world. Although he tried passionately to generate racing involvement amongst the car manufacturers of the 1920s and '30s, he was never to see the results of his endeavours. Within the social circles of the English high born young men of the time, who circulated around the various sporting scenes of car racing, horse racing or foxhunting, George, who was a motivator in the foxhunting world, knew Tim well and would have understood the sentiments of this man.

Edward De Burg Cantrell-Hubbersty

Edward, always known as Chang because he was nicknamed after a famous boxer who was touring the country at the time, was quite different from his two brothers. It was thought that he possibly got off to a bad start in life. Like Philip and George before him, he was sent to board at Eton College. After this he was unfortunately again sent away to stay with an old aunt and uncle in Buxton, who were rather staid. In retrospect the family now realise that this was misguided. He worked with his uncle in his solicitor's office in Buxton when he was only 19 years old but became very bored with the set-up. At night time, to liven up his life, he would climb out of his bedroom window and go down to the town to join in the local fun. In 1909 Chang, aged 27 years, was introduced to a local girl called Nell Leech by her husband Sidney. Foolishly Chang became involved with Nell, who, at 37 years of age, was 10 years his senior. Their secret cover was blown

Edward (Chang)
with his sister,
Augusta

when, at the Derby Club, Sidney overheard Chang speaking to Nell on the phone, saying, "I must go now as I am lunching with Sidney and if I remain any longer he will be suspicious. You know he suspects us now". Eventually, in August 1911, he was sited as co-respondent in a divorce suit, when it was discovered that during 1909 Nell and Chang had stayed together on several occasions for "an hour or two in a private room at a Temperance Hotel at Marchampton". Following this unfortunate turn of events, Chang had to do the honourable thing and marry Nell. The marriage was a disaster from the word go. They eventually had a legal separation but never divorced. Many years later a telegram arrived at the family home to say that Nell had died.

Unlike the rest of the family Chang did not like horses and therefore he did not go foxhunting. This alone would have been sufficient to exclude him from the main family circle. A further disadvantage was the fact that he had a speech impediment, which, it is thought, may have been the result of a lack of confidence due to his somewhat fractured upbringing. He continued to become entangled with a number of women who were quite unsuitable. He also continued to frequent the type of company that did not meet with the satisfaction of his family.

Quite shortly after Nell's death he met a girl called Gee, who was a hairdresser from Dorking and it is thought that this lady made him very happy. Through her influence he became a reformed character.

However Chang was simply unable to tell the truth. He always made up stories, so there was never any certainty about where he had really been or whom he had been with. Often these stories were told to get out of an imposed appointment, which he did not wish to keep. However the stories went further than that at times and on occasion were embellished for no apparent reason. Eventually later in life Chang resided with his elder sister Augusta's family, the Hales, for a good many years. During this time he was always a lot of fun for Augusta's children who never once saw him cross or grumpy - unlike his brother Philip.

Mary Frances Cantrell-Hubbersty

Mary Frances, known as Midget or Midge, was the youngest child of the family. She was nine years younger than her brother Chang. Born on the 24th of September 1891 at Felly Abbey, she was believed to be the result of an affair between the Earl of Harrington and her mother, Martha, during the previous hunting season. Within a short period of time, she moved with her family to Tollerton Hall. Her loving sister Augusta was married from Tollerton Hall in July 1898 when Midge was still only 6 years old before the family bought Ragdale Hall in 1908. Unfortunately, her mother disliked her greatly and during her earlier life, Midge was mostly kept in the schoolroom with endless governesses who themselves had varying levels of educational skills and abilities.

THE PEOPLE
**SHE'S RISING TO
THE OCCASION
-AND HOW !**

Some remarkable studies in expressions were caught by the camera at the Surrey Union Hunter Trials at Home farm, Mynthurst, Leigh, and this is how Miss Cantrell Hubbersty looked...

Midge in action

The only thing she was allowed to do that she liked, was to go foxhunting. If any punishment was administered it would be the withdrawal of the hunting favour. She was a fearless sidesaddle rider and drove her horse to jump a hedge as quickly as any of her male compatriots. On one occasion Midge was to tell the story of how she was looking forward to riding in the hunt on a horse on which she rode well. George, her brother, wanted the same horse and so he fabricated a story to her mother about something Midge was supposed to have done wrong. As a result her mother confined her to the house while George selfishly went out hunting on her favourite horse. Midge lived at Ragdale Hall until 1915, moving out when she was 24 years of age, in the same year of her father's death, to involve herself in the war effort and become a Land Girl.

So began a military career distinguished by the fact that she was one of the first women in the country to join the Land Army, later transferring to the Royal Flying Corps. It is thought that she went to France in connection with her war work as part of her photograph album includes snaps, which had been taken in France during the war years. She later returned to England to continue with her own life, which involved her great love of horses.

She had a sturdy character. In the early 1920s Midge moved to Kings Worthy in Hampshire and for several seasons hunted with the

THE TATLER

Mr. Rayson and Miss Cantrell Hubbersty

Tommy Rayson and Midge at the races

Hursley and Hampshire pack. By now her time was consumed by her greatest love, steeplechasing. For many years she rode out for Tommy Rayson, "who had some useful horses in training at Kings Worthy and who won the Grand National with Lovely Cottage in 1946" reported the Horse and Hound in her obituary of November 21st 1980. In those days women were rarely seen doing this kind of work and, like other ladies of her upbringing, she rode sidesaddle. However, to train horses she had to ride astride, which surprisingly, she found quite difficult to learn. In those times women were not permitted to hold a licence to train racehorses themselves but, when pony racing started up at Northolt in Middlesex, Midge became an enthusiastic owner and had several winners. "She virtually trained her own horses and, had the rules then permitted, would have taken out a licence". As she had been riding out for Tommy Rayson it would appear that Midge got Tommy to hold a licence on her behalf. She was therefore able to continue training horses and involve herself in the racing world to the extent that she would have done legally, if she had been permitted to be a trainer. Her niece, Pippa Woodroffe, remembers staying with her Auntie Midge and going out early in the morning to watch her on the gallops. Midge would then have been in her mid-thirties.

Midge also had a very interesting social scene as she was part of the Nottingham, Leicestershire and London "Sets" who kept company with Edward Prince of Wales and Freda Dudley Ward (nee Birkin). When Midge threw a party at her London address Edward, Prince of Wales attended. Both George and Midge were friends of the Birkin family. Freda Dudley Ward who was only two years younger than Midge was a famous society beauty who was associated with the Prince for many years before the advent of Lady Thelma Furness and finally Mrs. Simpson. Midge said that during Freda's relationship with the Prince of Wales her friend confided in her that, "although I am very fond of the Prince, he is not the love of my life". Freda was born on 28th July 1894 christened Winnifred May Birkin and she had two sisters, Vera and Violet. She was the eldest of the three daughters. Her father, Colonel Charles Birkin, was a prosperous lace manufacturer in Lamcote, Nottinghamshire. Col. Birkin was also Master of the South Notts Hunt in the 1920s. Freda married William Dudley Ward on 9th July 1913, two weeks before her 19th birthday. Her marriage to William, who was 16 years her senior, was finally dissolved in 1932.

George Cantrell-Hubbersty's friend Tim Birkin her racing driver brother, drove with Bentley and Bugatti and had a Bugatti team colleague, the Marquis de Casa Maury, who raced as Jacques Mones-Maury. It was through her brother Tim and the racing scene that Freda met the Marquis de Casa Maury, whom she married on 20th October 1937, now aged 43 years. This marriage lasted for some years before it was also dissolved in 1954. Remaining discrete about her affair with the Prince of Wales throughout her life, Freda died a few years after Midge in 1983, aged 88 years.

PER ARDUA AD ASTRA

The Aircorps Girls,
Midge third from left

Ragdale Hall remained the domain of Midge's eldest brother Philip with whom the family was generally not on very friendly terms. Their eldest sister, Augusta Margaret, was in contact with all of her family, but the rest of the siblings, especially George and Philip, had not related to each other well at all, mostly quarrelling over money issues. An interesting example of the level of estrangement is related in a short story from Midge. After some time of non-communication between them all, Midge met her brother Philip at a race meeting. Midge went up to Philip and said, "Hello Philip!" and he just grunted, so she said, "I am your sister Midge!" When he gave another grunt, Midge said, "Well we haven't seen each other for a good many years, have we?" Philip replied, "No I suppose we haven't." and cut any further possible conversation dead by simply walking away and that was the end of that!

In her latter years Midge lived at Westcott and was a well-known figure at Sandown and other steeplechasing meetings in the Southeast. Finally, her failing eyesight demanded that she could only follow her beloved racing by listening to the radio, but she lost none of her enthusiasm for the sport. Midge ran a large establishment right up until her death for, although she no longer kept horses herself, she had kept her stables open and nothing pleased her more than to have one or two horses in training liveried with her.

She was a very generous lady to all her family but she was rather frugal with herself, and would always look for, and delight in, a bargain, "to the point that she would wear shoes that hurt her if she got them as a bargain" fondly related her niece, Pippa Woodroffe (nee Hales). In her latter years she was an enthusiastic gardener. She died in 1980 at the age of 89 years. Although Midge lived to a fine old age, when she died she took with her the Cantrell-Hubbersty name, closing the book on the history of their family, many of whom were short-lived, and the 88 short years of the Cantrell-Hubbersty dynasty from 1892 to 1980.

Phyllis Cantrell-Hubbersty – "The Fairy Godmother"

Phyllis Cantrell-Hubbersty was very much a woman of her time. Before she became Mrs. Philip Cantrell-Hubbersty, she was Phyllis Mary Hermione Bethell. The wealthy Bethell family, were Squires in the 19th century, and as landed gentry had a very large estate in the East Riding of Yorkshire called Rise Park. Phyllis was the granddaughter of Lord Middleton and a cousin of the Willoughby family through her mother Marie Myrtle, who was Willoughby before marrying Phyllis's father William Bethell. Her father, Squire William Bethell, like his

WOMEN IN SPORT
THE HUNTING FIELD

The Duchess of Beaufort and Mrs. Cantrell Hubbersty; on foot, Lady Helena Fitzwilliam, at a meet of the Quorn

Phyllis on horseback predecessors, was a keen foxhunting gentleman with an income derived from the tenanted land he owned. Like Philip, Phyllis came from a strong foxhunting family background, the Bethell family having traditionally hunted with the Holderness Hunt. Phyllis married Philip Cantrell-Hubbersty in the early 1920s but, unusually for their time, they did not have children. Although not an avid rider like Philip, she rode sidesaddle and went out hunting with the local Leicestershire hunts after she married, especially riding with the Quorn.

Phyllis was around the same age as her sister in law Midge, but unlike Midge she wasn't really the typical sort of hunting personality, she did hunt and she understood all the hunting codes but she was more interested in interacting with people rather than chasing foxes. She was a lady of Edwardian standards, which was how she grew up, socialising around the many country houses. She circulated within the aristocratic and upper class social environment but, unlike many of those around her, she was aware of the changing face of the

Phyllis beside her
Rolls Royce

country, its times and its people. Phyllis was gifted with good common sense, and with her naturally outgoing personality she was a survivor, very capable of adapting to the changing times.

Phyllis Bethell had grown up with her brother Adrian Bethell at Rise Park. Adrian had followed in his fathers footsteps and on his return from the War became Master of the Holderness Hunt. Adrian had one child, a daughter Diana Bethell, by his first marriage to Clare Tennant. Unfortunately Adrian's marriage was not to last as Clare left Adrian and Diana to be with Lord Tennyson, grandson of the famous poet, resulting in Adrian and Clare finally divorcing. Lionel Hallam Tennyson was a fine sportsman and a cricketing star of his day. Born on 7th November 1889, he played for Hampshire County Cricket Club. He was voted Wisden cricketer of the year in 1914. After the First World War his career continued and he held the position of Hampshire Captain from 1919 to 1933, during which time he was Captain of England on three separate occasions. In 1928 he

succeeded as 3rd Lord Tennyson but he died quite young at the age of 62 on June 6th 1951. Lionel was known as a fun loving man with a great sense of humour. He did not take life seriously. Compared to Clare's first husband Adrian Bethell, who was a rather focused man who concentrated his energies on what he saw as his birthright, the survival of his estate and the Holderness Hunt in this post war era.

Adrian married again and went on to have two sons, Tony and Hugh, but unfortunately Diana's stepmother was unkind to her from the start and instilled a lack of confidence in the child, which was to undermine her for the rest of her life. Diana Bethell's father died in 1941, at the age of 50, following cancer of the lung, which was precipitated by a war injury. Diana's half brother Tony Bethell

inherited the family estate Rise Park upon his father's death. Diana went on to have two sons, David and Simon, by her husband Mr. Purcell Blow. Simon Blow is today a successful writer. The marriage did not last due to many factors, such as alcoholism and physical abuse and eventually Diana and Purcell divorced. This tragic mis-marriage effectively disenfranchised Diana from a secure future. Luckily her Aunt Phyllis was a giver. In the absence of Phyllis' brother Adrian and Diana's mother Clare, who never related to Diana, Phyllis stepped in to support her niece and two nephews, David and Simon Blow. She gave financial assistance and provided stability during their childhood. Simon Blow, describing his aunt, says, "Aunt Phyllie wasn't tough, she was stable, but not tough".

The Melton Toy Soldiers on parade

Like his father before him Philip was 16 years older than his wife, as was often the case in marriages of the period. Simon Blow tells us in his book Fields Elysian, that his Aunt Phyllis was in love with another before Philip came along. Victor, Marquis Conyngham of Slane Castle, County Meath, Ireland was her beau. An ancestor of Victor's, Lord Conyngham, was one of only two notable men who arrived at daybreak in June 1837 to inform the young new Queen Victoria that her Uncle, the King, had just died and that she was now Queen of the British Empire. Unfortunately Victor died of pneumonia during the First World War. However, even though Phyllis married Philip, she kept a photograph of Victor on her dressing table opposite a photograph of her husband. It would appear that Philip loved his wife even if the affection was not necessarily reciprocated.

In those days aristocratic girls were automatically disinherited from their family estate with the inheritance being transferred to the eldest male, so there was a pressure to "marry well" in order to survive within the system. Although the Ragdale estate was much smaller than Rise Park, Philip was sufficiently wealthy to provide Phyllis with a lifestyle to which she had become accustomed. It is felt that later on in life Phyllis may have had more private money than Philip and that her money may have gone someway towards supporting Ragdale Hall and the Quorn after Philip's death. In keeping with the class structure Phyllis was not necessarily wealthy from inherited family money but she had been left a variety of sums, from various maiden aunts, which contributed to her final wealth. Certainly upon her death her will was comparable in value to that left by Philip in 1947.

Phyllis had a terrific character. She was not beautiful but she had a ready smile for everyone and a terrific sense of fun. She was much admired for her *joie de vivre*. She ate heartily and as a result developed a rather matronly figure, which contributed to the perception of her being motherly and giving. Yet in many ways she was very feminine and brought a freshness to Ragdale Hall, which was sorely needed in those early days. She also had sound common sense and used it in abundance with her estate staff and in her community work. She adored delphiniums and would fill the Hall with enormous arrangements of these wonderful flowers, giving a highly scented aroma to the whole house during the season. Indeed she had a separate flower room where the main reception is located today. It is possible that Phyllis had a considerable intellect, because at some stage in her life she appears to have developed an admiration for the Scientist and Mathematician Sir Isaac Newton (1642-1727) who, in his day, had lived at Woodsthorpe Manor just beyond Belvoir Castle.

Helen Paulson often mentioned that Phyllis always wore a locket around her neck which contained some strands of his hair. Unfortunately whether Phyllis was interested in science or mathematics has not been discovered.

She was much loved by everyone in the community and even to this day, many years after her death in September 1962, she is remembered for her many kindnesses. Her nickname of the "Fairy Godmother" was repeated many times by those who remembered her. Phyllis was the sort of person who would help support local charitable needs. She would assist where she could to raise money by the provision of land for use as a venue or for a fete, allowing people to gather and contribute their efforts and money for a good cause. She was very much the Country Lady and as such was heavily involved with the community on a friendship basis. She made things happen for many people. She reached out to people in a way that Philip was simply not able to do. She really loved people and made them her friends. Due to this the community at large was devoted to Phyllis and would have done anything for her without stopping to consider any personal inconvenience. Although she was born into the aristocratic classes she had the ability to appeal to everybody and to work with them. She allowed no obstacle to prevent her from using her considerable resources for the betterment of all.

An early example of Phyllis' charitable enterprise occurred when, in 1925, the Hoby Women's Institute and Horticultural Society suggested building a village hall for Hoby, Rotherby, Brooksby and Ragdale, with a view to having somewhere to hold their meetings and the Annual Horticultural Show. She immediately offered Ragdale Hall as a venue for a summer fete in June of that year and the large sum of £260 (approximately £7,300 in today's money) was raised. A fete the following year, held at Earl Beatty's home at Brooksby Hall, raised £200 (approximately £5,600 in today's money). The Revd. Hugh Beresford, Rector of the parish, conveyed a piece of land in Hoby to four trustees and soon plans for the village hall were drawn up. By late autumn 1926 the hall was completed and on November 4th it was officially opened by Earl Beatty.

Between the wars, in 1932, Phyllis took on the position of Justice of the Peace for Leicestershire. She was perfect for the job; well respected and fair in her dealings with everyone. Always involved in the community events she sat on a number of committees. In 1935, as President of the Finance Committee of the Melton Mowbray Memorial Hospital (long before the commencement of our National Health Service on the 5th July 1948), she was successful when supporting advice by Mr Green, Treasurer to the Committee, to sell investments that had been put into stocks and shares for the benefit of the hospital capital funds, the sale realised a capital sum increase of £18,000, which in to-days money is equivalent to a staggering £450,000. Again her generosity reveals itself in the same year when she donated a Japanese table to a local auction held to raise money for local town amenities. Other prizes were two chickens from Lady Daresbury or a voucher of £4.00 (£100 today) from Colonel The Right Honourable J Gretton of Stapleford Hall.

During the Second World War Phyllis became Assistant Director of the Red Cross in Leicester taking on a high profile role supporting the work of the Red Cross and raising funds for the sorely needed Red Cross war support services. She placed herself in a hands-on staff position for the Red Cross Services and wore her uniform like the rest of the workers. She was a terrific organiser of people, especially in fund raising and was capable of injecting that special element into a function, which brought in the crowds and made an event a spectacular success. An example of this was her annual gymkhana event, organised to raise money for the Red Cross. This event was held throughout the war years at the back of the Hall and in front of the lake. She would have sideshows to hold and amuse the people and all sorts of Pony Club competitions. She was also able to arrange for one of her friends to attend with a private airplane to give aerial rides to those brave enough to take to the skies over Ragdale. Although something we may consider commonplace today, we have to remember that this was happening at a time when flight was still a rare experience. Such events stick in the minds of those who were lucky enough to be present. Phyllis also ran a shop in Melton Mowbray to support the Red Cross effort, the stores for which were kept in the Ballroom of Ragdale Hall. The beautiful Ballroom, reported to be "as long as a cricket pitch", was stacked high with the Red Cross first-aid supplies, wheelchairs, crutches and other equipment.

After the war she continued to devote her time to good works by sitting on the local bench as a Justice of the Peace and held the position of Treasurer to the Melton Toy Soldiers. Phyllis would open various bazaars and events for the community when requested, acting, and being treated as, a local celebrity.

When Philip died she was left to run the Ragdale estate entirely alone. Phyllis had been in Italy when her husband died and was unable to return for his funeral. The war had depleted all the large country houses of their staff and she had to use her ingenuity to find staff to keep Ragdale Hall and the estate farms operational. She turned

to the local Prisoner of War camp at Rotherby where a number of Italian prisoners were being held. She employed a number of these men to work on the estate. This turned out to be such a successful venture that, after the War, the Italian men eventually returned to their villages, seeking wives, only to return to England to continue working at Ragdale Hall until Phyllis left the area in September 1955.

After the death of her husband her other great concern was the Quorn Hunt which had depended so heavily for the previous seven years on its acting Master, Philip Cantrell-Hubbersty, for its finances and operation. Throughout its entire existence the Quorn Hunt had never had a woman Master of Foxhounds. However the hunt needed to act fast to ensure continued funding and this, which had been handled entirely by Philip, was no insignificant matter. Phyllis however, was an amazing woman and, with her practical approach to life and her natural teambuilding spirit, she changed Quorn history.

In 1948 she became the first woman ever to step into the Quorn male domain of Master of Foxhounds. She invited Fred Mee, a local

Phyllis with George Barker, Fred Mee and the Duke of Beaufort

*Ulrica Murray-Smith
at the beginning
of her 25 year
mastership*

farmer over whose land the hunt rode, to remain with her as joint master, together with the young Major, The Honourable Ronnie Strutt, who was later to become Lord Belper. Phyllis was a practical person, in this way she could share the workload of running the hunt, which was considerable, and also share the cost of such an undertaking. Phyllis had actually given up riding for a number of years before becoming Master, but her involvement made a valuable contribution to the hunt and gave it time to take stock, while the country struggled back to its feet in those post-war years. During this time she had a stable of about six hunters and a few racing mares. Phyllis would buy and sell her horses at Newmarket and there she made the acquaintance of a number of notable horse racing people of the time, including the Aly Khan. It is not clear whether she ever encountered Midge, while attending these horse racing events.

Philip had taken on the full maintenance of the Quorn Hunt himself, but this had been a full time job. Together with her duties to the Quorn, Phyllis had other activities she wished to continue, so the role had to be shared if she was to carry on her philanthropic interests. She was supported by the excellent and very experienced huntsman George Barker who commenced his 30 year term with the

SUPPLEMENT—1

COUNTRY LIFE

Vol. CXVII   No. 3048   JUNE 16, 1955

KNIGHT, FRANK & RUTLEY

By order of Executors.

LEICESTERSHIRE, CENTRE OF THE QUORN HUNT

Nottingham 15 miles, Leicester 12 miles, Melton Mowbray 6 miles.

A FREEHOLD RESIDENTIAL AND AGRICULTURAL ESTATE OF 376 ACRES

(Free of tithe and land tax.)

THE HOUSE is well situated on high ground, with extensive views.

Panelled hall, 4 reception rooms, panelled ballroom.

12 principal bed and dressing rooms. 3 bathrooms.

Nursery flat with 4 rooms and bathroom.

9 staff bedrooms, bathroom.

Self-contained flat.

Main electricity, power and water. Central heating.

5 COTTAGES (in hand).

THE LAND, which is in a ring fence, comprises 274 acres grass and 92 arable.

Main water is laid on to most fields. Woodland.

VACANT POSSESSION OF THE WHOLE

For sale as a whole privately, or by auction in lots, at a later date.

Joint Sole Agents: WILLIAM HARWOOD, Esq., Park Road, Melton Mowbray, and KNIGHT, FRANK & RUTLEY.   (13672 C.A.B.)

By direction of the Misses M. and S. Keyser.

SUFFOLK—CAMBRIDGESHIRE BORDER. NEWMARKET 7 MILES

The well-known Freehold Residential and Agricultural and Sporting

Quorn in 1929 and finished in 1959, when Lt. Col. G.A. Murray Smith finished his last season as Master. George Barker's expertise and experience acted as the bridge between the mastership of Philip and the new, shared mastership of Phyllis, Fred and Ronnie. When she resigned the post of Master in 1951 she was delighted that the mastership went to her great young friend, The Honourable Major Ronnie Strutt, who continued until 1954.

Phyllis led the way for women to be considered more credible as Masters of Foxhounds later on in the century. The redoubtable Mrs. Ulrica Murray Smith held the post for an amazing 25 years from 1960-1985. Phyllis also made the concept of shared or joint masterships acceptable so that hunts like the Quorn could survive in a fast-changing, tighter economy where money had much less value than in previous times. Phyllis Cantrell-Hubbersty has, to this day, an enormous reputation for being a warm, helpful person who had a terrific sense of humour. A kind and generous woman, she greatly assisted in the church renovation programme, which, at her request, ensured the re-opening of All Saints Church, Ragdale.

The Hall and Leicestershire represented a whole way of life with which she was familiar since she was a child and which was changed

Advertisement of sale, Ragdale Hall, 1955 and below: auction booklet

LEICESTERSHIRE
———
AN IMPORTANT TWO DAYS SALE OF A LARGE PORTION OF

THE CONTENTS OF RAGDALE HALL

MELTON MOWBRAY

BY ORDER OF MRS CANTRELL-HUBBERSTY

Thursday and Friday 21st and 22nd July 1955

(HSS)

61

forever when she sold the estate. It was brave for someone in her position to sell up and move away from all she knew when in her mid-sixties. The Hall was finally sold in February 1958, to Mr. Keightley.

On September 28th 1955, Phyllis moved to a beautiful small estate called "Peans Wood", situated in the picturesque village of Robertsbridge, Sussex. The property boasted a kitchen and scullery, china pantry, servants' hall, morning room, drawing room, dining room; sitting room, several bathrooms, eight bedrooms, two store rooms, three staff bedrooms and an attic. In all, a mini version of Ragdale Hall itself, which was about twice the size with fourteen guest bedrooms. Phyllis had a loyal following at Peans Wood as Luigi, her faithful chauffeur and general handyman moved with her to the new home, together with Fred Ward, her groom. In March 1958 Luigi married and it would appear that, like those before him, he worked with his wife on the Peans Wood estate, continuing to serve and support Phyllis as best he could. Phyllis acknowledges this in a letter written shortly after Luigi's wedding.

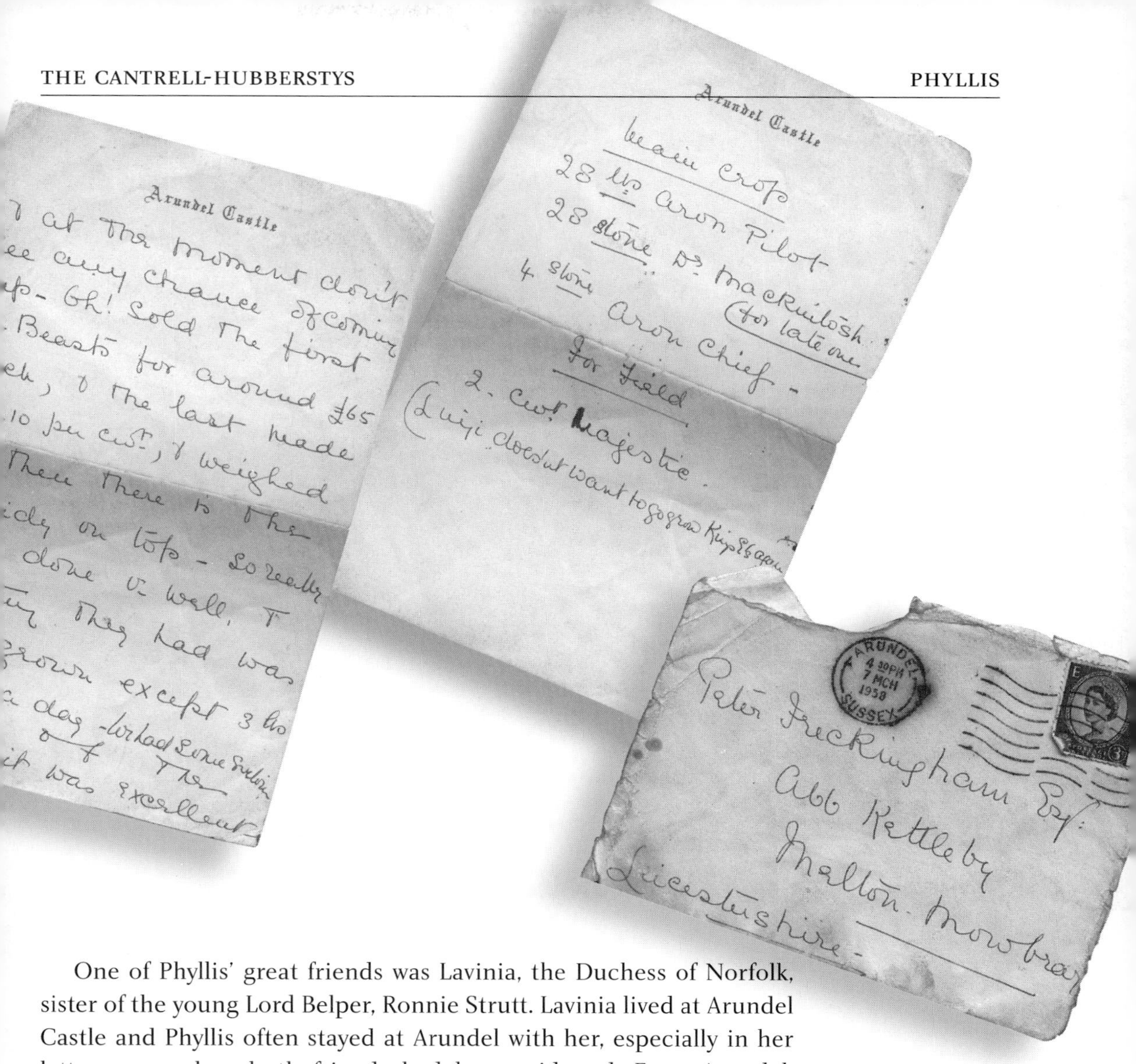

Arundel Castle

Arundel Castle

Main Crop
28 lb Aron Pilot
28 stone D. MacKintosh
                    (for late one
4 stone Aron Chief –

for field

2. cwt. Majestic.
(Luigi doesn't want to go grow Kip & gann

at the moment don't
ee any chance of coming
up – Oh! sold the first
Beasts for around £65
eh, the last made
10 per cwt, I weighed
Then there is the
dly on top – so really
done v. well, T
y they had was
grown except 3 tho
a day – or had gone rotten
out of the
it was excellent –

Peter Freckingham Esq.
Abb Kettleby
Malton Mowbray
Leicestershire

One of Phyllis' great friends was Lavinia, the Duchess of Norfolk, sister of the young Lord Belper, Ronnie Strutt. Lavinia lived at Arundel Castle and Phyllis often stayed at Arundel with her, especially in her latter years when both friends had been widowed. From Arundel, Phyllis continued to manage her estate, writing to those she trusted and who could help her organise the management of Peans Wood.

Illustrated above, a letter that Phyllis wrote from Arundel Castle, gives a clear idea of her concerns following her move to Peans Wood. Peter Freckingham, who lived at Home Farm, close to Ragdale Hall, with his wife Mary, was a trusted friend and an experienced farmer. Phyllis would turn to Peter for advice on certain estate matters. Peter Freckingham also helped her with the running of Peans Wood and, in her letter of March 7th 1958, she says:

"My Dear Peter, Have been meaning to write you, but it hasn't got done, then rang you last night, but got no reply, but wondered if you could come and stay next weekend, it would be so nice if you could, even you will find the trains 10 mins: to 20 quicker!! At the moment it

Opposite: Peans Wood and above, letter from Phyllis to Peter Freckingham, 7th March, 1958

63

Peans Wood
ROBERTSBRIDGE

About three-quarters of a mile from Robertsbridge Station on the Brightling Road.

Catalogue of

ANTIQUE AND MODERN

FURNITURE
including

Georgian D-end Dining Table, Set of Twelve Regency Dining Chairs,

A Pair of Louis XV Gilt Side Tables,

William Kent Table, Sheraton Sofa Table, French Kingwood Bureau, 18th and 19th Century Chests, Tables and Chairs, the Bedroom Furniture, Persian Rugs, Ornamental Items, China and Glass, etc.,

An 18th Century Ormolu Drum Clock,

A Pair of Sèvres and Ormolu Table Lamps, Meissen and other Figures, Silver and Plated Ware, Paintings, Water Colours and Engravings, Books, Wines, Linen, Curtains, including three Jacobean Bedspreads.

HAMPTON & SONS

---

will sell the above by Auction ON THE PREMISES

On MONDAY and TUESDAY,

26th and 27th NOVEMBER, 1962

at 11 a.m. each day

On View: Friday and Saturday prior, from 10 a.m. to 4 p.m.

Catalogues (6d. each) may be obtained from the Auctioneers:

HAMPTON & SONS,
6, Arlington Street, St. James's, London, S.W.1
Tel.: HYDe Park 8222 (20 lines)

And at *Wimbledon, Mayfield and Bishops Stortford*

is V. cold, came here (to Arundel Castle) yesterday till Monday; and will ring you in the evening. Now these are the potatoes they ask for on the enclosed paper, could you possibly get them, and could they be put on the train (passenger) insured as it won't cost any more than coming to fetch them and at the moment don't see any chance of coming up – Oh! Sold the first 2-beasts for around £65 each, and the last made about £7-10 per CWT, and weighed 9.1 (meaning 9.1 total CWT). Then there is the subsidy on top-so really have done, V-well. Everything they had was home-grown except 3lbs of cake, a dog – cooked some sirloin out of the Heifer and it was excellent. Have lots to show you and Thank Goodness so far Luigi seems as keen as ever and still making improvements. They came back 2 days after the wedding! He has certainly struck oil, she doesn't mind what she does, it helps in everything, do trust it goes on like that- now do come today next week. Many messages to all. (signed) Phyllis Cantrell-Hubbersty.

Listing the items she requires to be put on the train, she goes on:

Main Crops
28 lbs Aron Pilot
28 stone Dr Mackintosh (for late ones)
4 stone Aron Chief

For Field
2 CWT Magestic
(Luigi doesn't want to grow King Edwards again)

Compared to Ragdale Hall, Peans Wood was a smaller estate but it was run, like Ragdale, to support herself and her servants and produce enough of a surplus for her to entertain when she wished. Each winter, Phyllis treated herself to the healing waters fashionable at the time. She would travel to Italy staying either at the beautiful Marina Di Masa in Carrara, or at Montecatini Terme, both not far from Pisa, for up to three months of the year, thus sparing herself the cold English winter. It was while she was in Italy that the news arrived of her husband's death in March 1947. Normally a robust person even in her early seventies, Phyllis had developed shingles in England during the winter months of late 1961 and early 1962. Later that year, when holidaying again in Italy in September, she contracted hepatitis. She was transported back to London by airplane and although treated at the

Opposite, the auction booklet for Peans Wood, 1962

London Clinic, she could not be saved and died just one week later on September 8th 1962. Her funeral service was held at the little Parish Church of All Saints', Ragdale on September 13th 1962. Phyllis was buried beside her husband under the sundial which she had erected for him in 1947. Her death was upsetting for all who knew and loved her, not least for Diana Blow and her sons, David and Simon.

Former Quorn M.F.H. leaves £189,542

MRS. PHYLLIS MARY HERMIONE CANTRELL-HUBBERSTY, O.B.E., of Peans Wood, Robertsbridge, Sussex, formerly of Ragdale Hall, Joint Master of the Quorn Hunt 1947-51, former assistant director of the Red Cross in Leicestershire and a Justice of the Peace for Leicestershire, 1932, widow of Major William Cantrell-Hubbersty, O.B.E., D.L., a Joint Master of the Quorn—who died after a hunting accident in 1947—died on September 8 last, leaving £189,542 16s. gross, £183,433 13s. net value (duty paid £100,294).

She left £100 to her godchild Lord Lambton, "my red painted furniture" to Lord Guy Middleton, a dressing set to Lady Jane Bethell, an inlaid chest of drawers to the Hon. Mrs. Charles Lambton of Mortimer, Berks.

She left £2,000, an annuity of £65 and her Wolseley motor car, or such other car as he used in conjunction with farm as well as private work, to Luigi Loroire, and £250 to her former studgroom Frederick Ward in gratitude for their willing work "without any payment for overtime except harvest and hay money".

And £250 and an annuity of £65 to her parlourmaid Edith Bullock; £500 to Stanley Paulson, £250 to Peter Freckingham and £100 to Pat Scoley, employees; £100 to Mrs. McKerron, widow of her late chauffeur; £250 each to her former secretary Margaret James and former gardener Frederick Boddy; three months' salary, in lieu of notice, to each employee in her service at the time of her death of two years' service and upwards, and subject to their continuing their duties for one month, without salary, after her death if so required.

She left £200 upon trust for the upkeep of Ragdale All Saints' churchyard and a family grave; £250 to Leicester Old People's Evergreen clubs; £200 to the Royal Leicester, Leicestershire and Rutland Institution for the Blind; £200 to the British Empire Cancer Campaign.

£1,000 to Nancy Farquhar. £100 each to her godchild Victor F. McKeever, Anthony Bethell, Prudence Lane Fox, Elizabeth Peyton, Edward H. Brooke, Daphne Farquhar and Diana Blow, £500 each to the children of her nephew Richard A. Bethell, £200 each to the executors, her Rover motor car to her nephew David Blow, and, subject to other bequests of effects, the residue to be divided into 33 parts, as to 10 upon trust for her niece Diana Blow for life and then to her sons David and Simon.

Then to the said David Blow, five each to the said Simon Blow and said nephew Richard A. Bethell, and three to her nephew Christopher Bethell, or to their issue.

Probate has been granted to her nephew Richard A. Bethell of Rise Park, Hull, Yorks., and Gerald D. Adams, solicitor, of Selborne Buildings, Millstone Lane, Leicester.

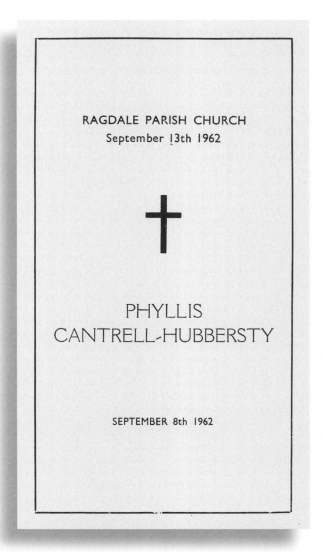

RAGDALE PARISH CHURCH
September 13th 1962

✝

PHYLLIS
CANTRELL-HUBBERSTY

SEPTEMBER 8th 1962

Right, Phyllis's funeral service booklet and above, details of her will

The contents of her home at Peans Wood in Sussex were auctioned at the house by Hamptons and Sons on Monday and Tuesday 26th and 27th November 1962 and the proceeds from the estate were divided among the family.

Phyllis's death heralded the closing years of an era which England would never be in a position to reproduce in the future. The financial demands of such a lifestyle are now largely prohibitive even to many of those born into wealth. The social changes, in the wake of two world wars, had alienated the old landlord system on which the Edwardian era depended for its survival. Phyllis seemed to know that these changes had to happen. Foxhunting had survived in many areas, despite many hunts collapsing during the war years. However foxhunting was to attract rising opposition from a nation becoming increasingly knowledgeable about such blood sports. Hunts were to become more nervous as anti-foxhunting campaigns grew nationally in scale and intensity.

The day was fast approaching when Ragdale Hall would no longer be involved in the hunting circle. Where commercial enterprise would supercede country seat and where the Monday Quorn importance would be a thing of the past for the owners of Ragdale Hall.

Ragdale Hall, 1955

Managing Through The Years

Surviving The Wars

It was in the years between the two World Wars that Melton Mowbray gained its greatest reputation as the most fashionable area in the country. The social life in the town at that time was legendary. Craven Lodge in particular was renowned for its parties, weekly shows put on by its lodgers and general high jinks that have left the townsfolk today with many stories of the high society capers linked to this phase in the town's history. Due to this social reputation the area attracted many notable people who not only visited for a day's hunting but also took up lodgings or rented a hunting box for a complete season of four months. On a regular basis people like Lady (Baroness) Ravensdale came to stay in Melton Mowbray, eventually buying her own house in the area. Also part of notable society were The Duke of Gloucester, residing at Warwick Lodge, the Duke of Rutland at Belvoir Castle, Lord Lonsdale at Saxelby Park Estate and Mr Robert Lowenstein, known as Bobby, at Satchville Cottage.

Bobby Lowenstein was a very wealthy untitled man who had an enormous stable of fine horses across the road from his home in the centre of the village of Thorpe Satchville. He was a keen sportsman and regularly took part in a variety of equestrian activities including hunting and polo. In some way he provided financial services to the hunting fraternity and was popular with the locals. Unfortunately he met with an untimely and tragic death in the early '20s when he disappeared flying his airplane across the English Channel.

In 1923, Edward, Prince of Wales, started to hunt from Melton Mowbray, riding out with all the hunts in the area. Often the Prince of Wales came to hunt, along with his two brothers Bertie and Henry which delighted the local townsfolk. The three Princes made an impressive sight and they took over a Royal Suite created for them at Craven Lodge, often using this as their base for the season. The estate owners surrounding the area were thrilled to be able to entertain the high society of London in their own country mansions. Ragdale Hall was no exception and, during this period, the Hall provided the venue for many important dinner parties, balls, and genteel gambling evenings for the Lords and Ladies, Dukes and Duchesses, Squires and Gentry, Maharajas and Maharanis who flocked to Melton Mowbray in great numbers to see and be seen.

Traditionally, estates like Ragdale had been financially stable until the introduction of Death Duty Taxes in 1894, followed by the introduction of Income Tax, both of which put new strains on wealthy families with large estates. This situation was exacerbated by the great loss of young male life in the First World War. At the beginning of the war the sons who normally inherited these estates were thrust into or volunteered for officer posts, often as raw recruits. However, as the army officer was often the first out of the trenches, these men were killed in great numbers. Subsequently estate trustees were often compelled to sell off huge slices of the estate to cover the enormous Death Duties. At the time there could have been little realisation of the incredible process of change the First World War would begin within the country, its class system and its politics.

The Second World War, following on before the economic revival had been completed, signed the death knell for the lifestyle represented by estates like Ragdale Hall. To make matters worse, in the Second World War many of the beautiful grand houses were confiscated by the War Office, sometimes with as little as a week's notice, to be used as barracks for troops. When the houses were finally returned to their owners a few years later, many were in such a dilapidated state that the owners simply could not find the enormous funds the refurbishment operation would require and the only solution was to abandon or demolish them.

A clear example of this is the Shirley family seat of Staunton Harold, which was requisitioned by the army for troops and later for the housing of Italian prisoners of war. When the house was handed back, many family treasures had been lost or trashed and the house was in such a state of disrepair that Earl Ferrers was unable to re-occupy it. In the absence of adequate compensation they decided to sell. On the eve of the auction on 11th October 1954, the 12th Earl Ferrers died, it is said, of a broken heart. Shortly after the sale the purchaser announced his plans for the demolition of the Hall. A preservation order gave a six-month stay of execution but no use could be found for the Hall until, with only five weeks to spare, Group Captain Leonard Cheshire made an offer to purchase it for use as a Cheshire Home for disabled people. Today Staunton Harold Hall is still actively occupied by the Ryder-Cheshire Mission.

At other such great Halls, where renovation was viable, the cost of doing so, without any post-war government money to assist the owners, meant an uncertain future for many of these houses. Now put into context, Ragdale Old Hall was just one of many similar large old houses at that time, for which there was no money for renovation, even though there may have been value in its heritage. It seems that the new Ragdale Hall was lucky not to have been confiscated by the War Office. However, it is believed that at the end of the Second World War, the American soldiers of the 101st Parachute Regiment spent some time on the estates acreage preparing for the D-Day landings.

By 1940 the former Victorian affluence that England had enjoyed had dwindled to a trickle of spare cash available only in certain corners of the country. Many of those who were financially better off were more reticent to display their wealth as much as in former times. The country was changing. People were more informed through the media, of the lifestyle differences between the classes. Rationing had been introduced. Opposition to foxhunting increased considerably and it became less fashionable to be overtly affluent and involved in such blood-sporting pastimes. The numbers of landed gentry with tenanted farmers were reducing dramatically. The remnants of the old feudal system were disappearing forever. Differences between the classes were to become less apparent over the next fifty years. Any activity that required high funding was apt to go into decline as the country tried to pull itself back on to its feet. Foxhunting was no exception to this. Without the large numbers available to hunt (in former times it was not unknown for 400 or more to go out with a pack of hounds) the subscriptions fell away and in many cases the hunt closed. This was the situation that faced the Quorn hunt in 1940 and this is what Philip Cantrell-Hubbersty dealt with in the only way he knew how - by funding the hunt himself. In those days there was a certain sense of honour in being able to fund a hunt without help - after all this was the norm in the previous century. However, even in 1940, it was recognised that without the support of high numbers of subscriptions, Philip had taken on an enormous financial burden which undoubtedly ate into his considerable wealth and may have been a factor in the ultimate selling of Ragdale Hall only eight years after his death. There is no doubt that, from the start, Phyllis was mindful of expenditure after her husband's death.

The House in the '20s, '30s and '40s

At the turn of the century Ragdale Hall was managed along the lines of a very grand Victorian family home. The Ragdale estate was totally self-supporting, as was the case for all such estates of this kind. During the '20s the whole estate was highly staffed to support the many visitors who would stay at the Hall. In the house there was a butler, two footmen, a head housekeeper, several chambermaids, several housemaids, a cook, several kitchen staff, a chauffeur and an under chauffeur. From the mid-'20s the stables were run by Mr. Ward, head groom, an under groom and several stable hands, not to mention the stable hands who travelled with their visiting gentry.

At night a small number of staff stayed on duty to respond to the needs of the family or guests. Charles, the butler had his Butler's

Chair, which stood in the main hallway beside the front door. He was always pristinely turned out in his crisp butler's uniform and white kid gloves which he always wore while on duty and had that air of command particular to butlers of the period. The footmen also had their uniform but wore green baize aprons when doing some of the dirtier jobs, such as cleaning the silver in the butler's pantry. The house had to be able to support the many dinners and balls that were very much part of the social scene. In keeping with the position of the Cantrell-Hubberstys in this fashionable society, Ragdale Hall was for years the natural venue for the annual Quorn Hunt Ball which was always well attended by all the high society of London.

All housework had a strict routine. This enabled the Cantrell-Hubberstys to portray a superior well-run house and stables to all their guests. At times these guests were notable indeed and the scandal attached to their lives made national headline news. Prince Edward reportedly stayed at the Hall several times in the '20s with his brothers and later, in the '30s, he returned to visit with Mrs Wallis

Simpson. Sydney Panter was butler at this time and often served the Prince during his stay. He reported that the Prince was extremely fussy about how his bacon was grilled for breakfast as "it had to be just right!" Sydney, who lived in Ragdale Village in the mid-'30s, was a freelance butler who followed the aristocratic families around during the various hunting seasons, such as grouse shooting in Scotland. He also provided batman services to other famous people such as Izzi Bonn the entertainer. Due to his close proximity to the upper-class set at Ragdale Hall and Craven Lodge, Sidney was one of the few people who knew of the liaison between The Prince of Wales and Mrs. Wallis Simpson before the news became public. Sidney related how the Prince had met Mrs. Simpson in 1933 when introduced to her by Lord and Lady Furness while out in the gazebo at the bottom of the garden at Burrough Court. Lady Thelma Furness (also American) was mistress to the Prince at this time. In early 1934 Lady Furness asked Wallis to look after the Prince in her absence while she visited the United States for a couple of months. By the time she returned Wallis had well and truly endeared herself to the Prince to the point that her position was immoveable. The Prince's chauffeur, while in Leicestershire, was a local man, Mr Tom Webster. What could not have been foreseen was that the liaison between Prince Edward and Wallis Simpson, which flourished in the beautiful Leicestershire countryside, was to change the course of British history.

The Cantrell-Hubberstys had their different domains of control. Responsibility was shared; all internal work was managed by Mrs. Cantrell-Hubbersty and all external work was the responsibility of 'The Major'. Whole families were employed on the estate. Most of them also lived either in accommodation at the Hall or in cottages on the estate land making a high number of people dependent on the estate.

Room layout at Ragdale Hall in 1935 was as follows:-

Ground Floor: Library, dining room, main hall, strong room, flower room (Mrs. Cantrell-Hubbersty's personal room known as the boudoir), lounge, inner hall, ballroom.

First Floor: Major's bedroom, breakfast room, Mrs. C-H's bedroom, main guest suite (room 6) 8 remaining guest rooms all with dressing rooms, 3 bathrooms and toilets, linen cupboard.

Second Floor – The Nursery: The nursery consisted of four main rooms and a few smaller rooms.

The Tower Room: 1 bedroom, a Westminster chiming clock by J. Smith and Sons of Derby, and 6 large galvanised water storage tanks.

Servants Wing – Ground Floor: Housekeeper's room, butler's pantry, boot room, kitchen, scullery, back stairs up to the servants quarters, dustbin area, back door, laundry.

Servants Wing – First Floor: 12 servants bedrooms, servants bathroom and toilet, housemaids closet.

The Gardens

The gardens were tended by two gardeners, a senior, Mr. Fred Boddy in the early '30s, followed later by Mr. Stanley Paulson, and an under gardener who was possibly Mr. Paulson's son. The two gardeners really had their work cut out for them as all of the land in front of the Hall, known as "The Park", was cultivated with trees right down to the village of Ragdale. This entire area of parkland from the Hall to the village was kept neatly cut and tended. It was through this area that the front

Stanley Paulson, Head Gardener in the late '30s

drive rose elegantly out of the village and came up to the Hall in an enormous sweep around the front gardens, to terminate at the front door under the protective stone canopy, which carries the family crest.

The Stables

Fred Ward,
Head Groom
with horses in
the paddock

One senior groom, Mr. Fred Ward and several stable hands, staffed the stables. They had to support the turnaround of mares required for hunting as well as riding backup horses to and from the locations at the hunt. The house had to be able to accommodate large numbers of guests arriving for the hunt. The stables provided any guest who wished to hunt on a given day, a well bred and well turned out mare for the occasion. Therefore they needed to accommodate several good horses, surplus to the family requirement. The stables were large enough to accommodate guests' own horses if required - a provision expected by guests as part of the hospitality of the house. Philip and Phyllis ran a fully functioning stable yard which included breeding their own stock of horses at the Ragdale Hall stables. These horses were subsequently raised at Ragdale for racing, buying and selling at Newmarket. Philip, in particular, was well known among the horseracing fraternity.

Farm and Estate Produce

With its several thousand acres and two farms, the estate generated sufficient crops, beef, pork, lamb, poultry, milk, cheese and eggs,

vegetables, herbs and flowers to support the family, guests and their considerable staff. The land staff were headed up by Mr Fred Boddy. The poultry and the piggeries were ably managed by Mr. George Buck and caring for the sheep in the fields was the responsibility of Mr. Warnes, the shepherd, who lived with his wife in a small cottage on the estate. The estate staff made a small community which was naturally inter-dependant and completely self-supporting.

Tommy Cox with three maids in the hay in the '30s

Life between the wars for the Ragdale Estate staff reflected the rural way of life of many other large estates around the country. The staff were more like an extended family unit and shared their fortunes and misfortunes together. Cook took it upon herself to mother and protect, as much as she could, the young 14 year old girls who arrived at Ragdale Hall to be housemaids. Often having just left home and school for the first time. She encouraged them to write home on a frequent basis. She was a strict disciplinarian and regularly doubled as a chaperone as required.

Utilities

The estate generated its own electricity supply. The Hall got its power from a generator, which powered up a large number of storage batteries. Garners of Melton serviced the Hall's storage battery cells. These cells were large - about 2 feet square – and filled with electrodes. It was Garners' job to check the specific gravity of the electrolyte in the cells and to ensure that they had not sludged up over time. There were a total of 54 cells in one battery room and they would be changed as required, on an annual basis. Over the doorway into this battery room there was a bank of the old Leclanché cells running the houseroom bells which the family and guests would use to call the servants from the servants' Hall. The generator ran for two days a week and this created enough power to run the Hall for the rest of the week. In the '30s the Hall had a chauffeur called William who also had a junior driver called Tommy Cox. It was William's responsibility to check the generator but, as he was always dressed in a blue serge suit and kid gloves, William would prefer to call Garners to come and sort out any problem as soon as possible.

*Tommy Cox, left,
and Fred Boddy,
centre, 1930s*

In around 1910 the Garners man for Ragdale Hall was Earnest Waplington and later on in the '30s it was Earnest's son, Neville Waplington, continuing at Garners in his father's footsteps.

The estate also had its own water supply which was extracted from two wells located about 400 yards from the Hall, Garners again servicing the water supply services to the Hall. Water storage tanks were located in the clock tower. There were two 500-gallon tanks held there and these had an indicator on the side of each tank to show how much water they were holding at any one time. The tanks were filled with water from the two wells. There was a deep well, which had a drop of 83 feet before it reached the water table and from which very clear water was extracted. A shallow well, which was contaminated with surface water, delivered water which was not so pure. The two wells were used alternately to mix the water so that it still maintained an acceptable quality for use in the house. This water was pumped up from the two wells to the tanks in the house. Any surplus water was turned into the moat to top it up. For this there was a special valve which released water into the moat. The main reason for using both wells was that in the summer months the deep well could run dry, while water was still accessible from the shallow well. The deep well had a barrel-shaped curved bottom and this would sometimes silt up in the summer when the water table fell during the drier months. The alternating of these wells allowed the deep well to recover in the dry months. Unlike other large houses in the area, there was never a water shortage at Ragdale Hall. The deep well never had a gas problem but surprisingly the shallow well did have gas present at times. Unlike modern Health and Safety procedures, breathing apparatus was not used in those days to protect maintenance staff against gas in this kind of confined space. The way they dealt with this hazard was quite primitive. Gas was detected by dropping dry straw down the well and setting fire to it. The gas was burnt off, and an upward rush of hot air from the fire pushed out any residue of gas, causing a vacuum. Then the well cavity was naturally refreshed with cold fresh air that rushed in to fill the vacuum. About an hour after this procedure was carried out it was safe for men to enter the well.

The Hall had its own water-filled radiator, central heating system as far back as 1935, when Neville Waplington first worked with Garners. The two main boilers and the coke for the boilers were located in the cellar. Boiler number 1 was for domestic water and number 2 was for the central heating. The central heating was furnished by large Victorian radiators, which had huge fins to deliver the heat to the high ceiling rooms.

*Mr and Mrs
Earnest Waplington*

One emergency call to Garners was sent following a catastrophic flood, resulting from the heating system freezing up during the winter. Two of the radiators under the windows in the Lounge (then the ballroom) had burst and spilled water all over the carpets. The resulting flood was enormous and continued into the cellars, flooding them to a foot deep. By the time Neville answered the call and entered the cellars, he found them flooded to a depth of more than three feet. After a struggle to find the drainage outlet, he resolved the problem and succeeded in releasing the flood water. Apart from damage to flooring and carpets, the house was eventually returned to normal.

*Neville
Waplington*

Staff in the '30s

The house staff in the '30s were always friendly and tried the best they could to work together as a team. The kitchen staff was headed by Mrs. McKerron who was a talented cook and who had met her husband at Ragdale Hall when he was the Cantrell-Hubbersty's head chauffeur. She managed a small team of three kitchen staff, two kitchen maids and a scullery boy. Mrs. McKerron was not noted for her personal presentation but she had great ability when putting on a grand dinner for the Cantrell-Hubberstys, complete with wonderful sauces and exquisite garnishes. Dinner parties were not large. However when they

*Sidney Panter
in his livery*

did entertain, the dinners were amazing. Due to Mrs. McKerron's skills the Cantrell-Hubbersty's would feast on saddle of lamb with kidneys, fried and bread crumbed, arranged decoratively down the sides of the joint, with exotic vegetables like asparagus and beans, even when they were out of season. There would always be a fancy starter and a delicious dessert or pudding. Mrs. McKerron was exceedingly good at making everything look so exquisite for the formal occasion. For this she was much admired among the kitchen staff.

The Major did not seem to have an extensive cellar but he had a good selection of fine wines which his butler, Mr. Panter, was

*Mr and Mrs Sidney
Panter at the top
of the Hall drive*

responsible for matching to the foods being served at dinner.

Betty Cartwright (nee Short) started working at Ragdale Hall as first kitchen maid in 1934 when she was 14 years old, assisting in general duties until just after the outbreak of war in 1940. Her friend Lorna Jackson (nee Hodgson) commenced as second kitchen maid in 1935 when she was 15 years old, assisting in general duties and serving to the breakfast room on the 1st floor located between the Major and Mrs. Cantrell-Hubbersty's bedrooms. Lorna also left Ragdale Hall in 1940. Both girls came from Halfway School in Halfway Village, Derbyshire. They had been friends at school, had grown up together remaining friends until Betty's recent passing. On the day they arrived at Loughborough to commence work at the Hall they were met by Mr. McKerron, the head chauffeur, in the Rolls Royce and taken to Ragdale Hall. A ride in a motorcar was a rare experience in itself, but to ride in a Rolls Royce was well worth writing home about and they did just that. The only other time the girls would ride in the Rolls Royce was once a month on Sunday's when they were driven down to Ragdale to attend church.

When the girls went home to visit their families they would either be driven to Broughton Station in one of the Ragdale cars or they would cycle to the station. Leaving their bicycles there, they would travel on by train to Killamarsh, the station nearest to their home. Finally they would walk the last mile, as there were no buses on the final part of the route.

Kitchenmaids Betty Cartwright and Lorna Jackson with housemaids Joan Scearton and Ada Toon on the old engine room windowsill, 1936

House Routine in the '30s

The old clock in the tower chimed the Westminster chime every 15 minutes throughout the 24-hour day. Often the girls would waken early in the morning only to be reassured by the chime that it was only 5:00am and it was not yet time to get up. The day started at 6:30am but, as the housemaids had to be up earlier than the kitchen maids, they would put on the lights in the kitchen. As a result the kitchen staff often had an extra sneaky half hour in bed and would not get up until 7am. At this time of the morning the hot water bottles would be

Housemaids Hilda Windsor, Joan Scearton, and May Green visiting Willoughby in 1939

fetched from the bedrooms and the Major and Mrs. Cantrell-Hubbersty would be served their first cup of tea of the day. Then it was the duty of the first kitchen maid to make the brown scones, toast and marmalade which the Major and Mrs. Cantrell-Hubbersty had every morning for breakfast. This was prepared in the early days on a black leaded range and later on an Aga style stove made by Crittal of Nottingham. As a second kitchen maid, Lorna had her work cut out for her as her duties included assisting with the washing up, scrubbing the surface boards and floor cleaning. The scullery, the stone Hall, the long servants' wing passage, the housekeeper's room, the dairy, and the butchery were all scrubbed by Lorna on her knees.

Meal times for the family and guests were strictly adhered to. Breakfast was served every morning from 8:45am in the upstairs breakfast room. However Phyllis and Philip did not often eat breakfast together. The Major would have his breakfast at 8:45am and then prepare for the day's meet scheduled for 11am. He would leave the Hall accompanied by his groom and a second horse. Phyllis on the other hand did not necessarily get up that early and her daily schedule was often quite different to the Major's. Breakfast was taken on trays, directly from the kitchen by the kitchen maids, to the guests' rooms. This would be a cooked English breakfast or sometimes kedgeree. A light lunch was served at 1:15pm and the main meal of the day was dinner in the evening. Dinner, served at 8pm, would be attended by Mr. Panter, the butler and a housemaid in her red and coffee uniform especially worn for the dining room. Dinner was served for the Cantrell-Hubbersty's in their dining room even when they were alone. A typical meal when the Major and Phyllis were on their own for dinner during the week was a simple affair of possibly roast chicken or steamed fish. At weekends a large beef joint would be cooked to feed both the Cantrell-Hubbersty's and their house staff. All house servants ate their meals in the servants' hall and they would be served a cooked breakfast on a regular basis. Following dinner in the servants' hall the housemaids would either read or listen to the radio in the housekeepers' room before going to bed around 10pm.

But not all was work, work, work. They also had some playtime. The Tower had the most beautiful view and often, when the Cantrell-Hubbersty's were away from the Hall, the two young girls would climb up the narrow staircase and onto the roof to gaze at the fantastic view. On a clear day one can see panoramic views for up to 30 miles.

When the ice cream man, Mr. Charlie Wyard, arrived on his bicycle on a weekly basis and stopped at Six Hills, the girls would fetch some ice cream for themselves and sit out on the old engine house windowsill to eat it. It was the same with the lollypops that Jean Todd held in store for them, they would take a break and sitting in the garden they would laugh and chatter and eat their ice lollypops.

Their time off was very little - just a half day per week. Their busy timetable allowed only a Sunday morning off one week and a Sunday afternoon the next. Time off for the staff comprised of cycling the 6 miles to Melton Mowbray, leaving their bikes at Garners, going to the pictures during the day and cycling back to the Hall to be in before the curfew time of 9:45pm. They didn't even have time for a cup of tea and a bun before they returned. When they went to Leicester however, they travelled by bus and relaxed with a cup of tea and beans on toast out of their 10 pennies before returning to the Hall.

When Phyllis Bethell married Major Cantrell-Hubbersty in the early 1920s and moved to Ragdale Hall she brought three members of her own staff from Rise Park with her. They were Nanny Irving, Jean Todd housekeeper, and Fred Boddy head gardener, and they were to form the core of her staff in her new home. Due to her friendly and encouraging nature, Phyllis was never going to encounter problems when recruiting and retaining key staff to help her in various aspects of estate management. A good example of this was her personal maid, Jean Todd who assisted her for more than forty years and of course Mr Fred Boddy, head gardener who was with her for about thirty years.

House staff
Mr. Sidney Panter - *Butler*
Mr. George Lawson – *Footman*
Mr. McKerron – *Head chauffeur*
Tommy Cox - *Under chauffeur*
Nanny Irving (who had been nanny to Diana Blow in previous years)
Jean Todd – *Head housekeeper and personal maid to Phyllis*
Edith Bullock – *Parlour maid*
Ada Toon - *Housemaid*
Joan Scearton – *Housemaid*
Mrs. McKerron – *Cook*
Betty Short – *First kitchen maid*
Lorna Hodgson – *Second kitchen maid*

Land staff
Mr. Fred Boddy – *Head gardener*
Mr. Garner – *Under gardener*
Mr. Buck – *Pig and poultry man*
Mr. Pat Scoley – *Cattleman*
Mr. Warne – *Shepherd.*

Stable Staff
Fred Ward – *Head Groom*
Pat Scoley – *Under Groom*

"THE LEICESTERSHIRE SET" 1931

Major Harbord	Major W. P. Cantrell-Hubbersty	Major J. F. Harrison	Lord Carnarvon	Major-General John W
'Joe'	Miss E. Paget	Miss Monica Sherriffe	Major Metcalfe Mr Ambrose Clarke	Major C
Captain de Pret	Mr D. E. Johnstone Lady Ravensdale	Sir Harold Nutting, M.F.H.	Major A.E. Burnaby, M.F.H.	The Hon. Mrs. Gilbe

"The Leicestershire Set" caricatured for 'The Tatler' in 1931, featuring Major Cantrell-Hubbersty and Lady Ravensdale

Jean Todd was very close to all the central operations of the house and as Phyllis' personal maid she knew everything that was going on at the Hall. She could be great fun often joining the staff on the piano in the Ball Room. Her housemaid team consisted of Joan Scearton and Ada Toon, who married the Ragdale Hall under chauffeur Tommy Cox. The house had a full-time butler Mr. Sidney Panter and footman Mr. George Lawson. A little later on in the '30s the team was joined by another two housemaids – reflecting the growing demands of the Cantrell-Hubbersty's social scene.

Mr. Fred Boddy, the head gardener, who lived in the cottage near the main entrance, led the land staff. Mr. Garner, the under gardener, would pop in every morning with the fruit and vegetables for the day and have a quick coffee before he left. Mr. Buck, the pig and poultry man, lived with his wife in one of the semi-detached houses along the drive. Mr. Pat Scoley was the cattleman and Mr. Warne the shepherd.

There were a lot of visitors who came to stay at Ragdale for short stays throughout the hunting season. Lady Ravensdale (Irene Curzon), a great friend of Phyllis's, was passionate about hunting in Leicestershire. Irene came on a regular basis throughout the '30s and she would always stay in the main guest room (now room 6) as a houseguest. In those days this room was called the Blue Room. Mrs. Fiddler was her lady's maid and she also had a chauffeur called Tom. Other rooms were called after fruits, such as the Apricot Room with the bow window overlooking the rose garden. There was the Brown Room, and the Orange Room and the Little Blue Room, which was the drinking room. The Duke of Gloucester was another frequent visitor to the Hall together with Edward, Prince of Wales, "who was very fussy with his food" reported the butler Mr. Panter. Diana Blow and her children David and Simon stayed at Ragdale Hall periodically during this time. His sister Rita periodically visited Philip. However Philip's younger sister Midge never came to the Hall between 1934 and 1940, presumably as a result of the rift between herself and Philip.

It is reported that the Duke of Norfolk met Lavinia Strutt, the daughter of Lord Belper, at Ragdale Hall. Lavinia and her brother Ronald were very close friends of Phyllis's and they kept in frequent touch through their lives. Lavinia later married the Duke and become the Duchess of Norfolk. Subsequently Phyllis often stayed with the Duke and Duchess at their home, Arundel Castle.

Staff in the '40s and '50s

Married staff working at the Hall always enjoyed rent-free cottages in the grounds of the estate while single staff had free accommodation in the servants' wing at the Hall. All food and provisions from the estate were absolutely free for the families of everyone who worked in or around the entire estate. Their good employers covered all their health requirements. In Phyllis Cantrell-Hubbersty's case, when her staff required a medical opinion, she often referred them to her own physicians in Melton Mowbray or Harley Street. Their journey to the physician was either in the spare car, the Ford, or by chauffeured Rolls Royce. Although the Rolls Royce was usually kept for the Cantrell-Hubbersty's exclusive use, the Ford was often lent to any member of the staff who could drive, for their days out.

By 1940 most able bodied and willing people in the community had left and gone overseas to war or were involved in the war effort. Philip and Phyllis lost most of their house and land staff at this time. Lorna and Betty returned to their village Halfway, to be with their families and the men joined the army. Consequently during the years of the Second World War there were very few skilled people available generally in the country, the Melton Mowbray area was no exception to this. The Cantrell-Hubbersty's relied heavily on a supply of men from the Italian Prisoner of War Camp at Rotherby to staff the estate. These prisoners had been transported from the continent following capture by British troops and were in safe holding until the declaration of peace. As man power they were released out to local estates to assist with land duties.

Luigi Loreire with Mary and Peter Freckingham

One such prisoner of war was Luigi Loreire who became the main support to the house and grounds. He was the type of man who could turn his hand to anything and did so to help Mrs. Cantrell-Hubbersty with her estate. Luigi became her estate manager, chauffeur and, on many occasions, her personal advisor on staff matters. He was a man much respected by all staff whether they worked within the household or based on the land.

By now the team of people at Ragdale had changed. During the years between the '40s and early '50s the staff at the Hall had dropped dramatically to 13 people and the estate was almost completely staffed by remaining members of families who had worked with the Cantrell-Hubbersty's for many years and Italian men and their wives.

House staff in the late 1940s and early 1950s

Margaret James – *Personal secretary*
Jean Todd – *Head housekeeper and personal maid for 40 years*
Edith Bullock – *Parlour maid*
Luigi Loreire – *Chauffeur and general assistant*
Tranquilla Baldo – *Cook*
Antonietta Polliono – *Housemaid and cleaner*
Maria Santoro – *Housemaid*

Gardeners

Stanley Paulson – *Head gardener*
Graham Ward – *16year old trainee gardener (Fred Ward's 3rd son)*

Some of the Italian staff including 4th from left to right Tranquillo Baldo, Maria Santoro and her husband Cosimo

*Tranquilla Baldo
by the rear
entrance of
the Hall*

Stables
Fred Ward – *Head groom and stable manager*
Pat Scholey – *Under groom*
Gordon Ward – *Stable boy (Fred Ward's 2nd son)*

Farms
Cosimo Santoro – *Farm hand*
Emilio Polliono – *Farm hand*
Pasquari – *Farm hand*

Maria Santoro
by the main gates,
showing the old
entrance pillars

The Decline of the Acreage

The Ragdale estate started to break up during the war years. To suit the hunting passion of the Major his total acreage had been left entirely to grass prior to the war, but the War Agricultural Committee demanded that the grass acres of this quality land be turned to arable so that crops could be grown to support the war effort. Cecile Earl was a farmer who the War Committee had appointed to oversee, amongst others, the Ragdale Hall Estate lands conversion to arable. This really upset Major Cantrell-Hubbersty and the surrounding hunting community who relied so heavily on the land remaining as grass to continue with their sporting activities. The Major appealed, but it made no impact on the War Agricultural Committee and Mr Cecile Earl was here to stay. He ran the farm half way down the hill, which belonged to the Ragdale Estate, and as his residence he occupied Home Farm in the village.

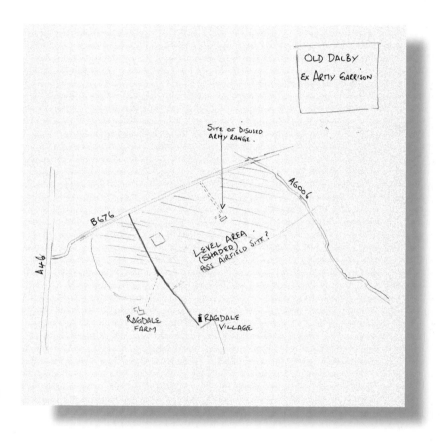

Hand drawn map of the landing site – Ragdale (1) courtesy of Mr Bill Clarke

Around the same time in early 1942 another war effort threatened the Ragdale Estate acreage, this time from the Air Ministry. Both the Air Ministry and the Ministry of Agriculture and Fisheries were locked in a battle of their own, over the use of land for food production as opposed to provision for airbase activity essential for the war. It had been recognised by Government that the country needed to acquire sufficient airfields to meet the needs of increasing flight operations to and from the continent, together with the necessity to provide emergency landing ground to cope with flights returning low in fuel or unable to reach their airbase due to damage incurred in battle. The

Fred and Ellen Ward outside their cottage at the Hall, 1951

geographical flatness of the region lent itself to building such an airfield base. Other considerations being made were to accommodate the need for increased training units to be established across the country. Operational Training Units or OTU's as they were known, were springing up rapidly in an effort to get the flight crews trained and ready for war as quickly as possible. This included bomber training as well as target training.

The Air Ministry were also frantically trying to find a suitable satellite site for the technical airbase Wymeswold without utilising good arable land greatly needed for milk and crop production to support the war effort. Castle Donnington had been identified as a possibility for a bomber aerodrome, but the area was excellent arable land and the 460 acres available were already producing for the coming harvest. At this stage the two other sites under consideration were Ragdale and Derby. Ragdale had proved to be undesirable but not impossible to develop primarily from a construction point of view, as it was a "Green Field Site" and the cost of development and time factor involved, would have been considerable. Derby on the other hand was not ideal either, as it was in use as an Elementary Flight Training School (EFTS) and as such was providing an increasingly essential service. Ragdale had two useful sites identified by the Air Ministry. Ragdale (1) had already been used for target training by the army, in the large field bordering the B676 and A6006 where the reservoir is now located. Again Ragdale (1) was also where an Emergency Landing Ground or (ELG) had been identified and the Air Ministry had wished to expand this site in the summer of 1941 but were unable to do so, as alternative accommodation for another army firing range could not be found. Ragdale (2) selected in January 1942 was where the development of East Midlands Airport may so easily have taken place. This second site was the larger percentage of the estate that was sufficiently flat to accommodate take off, landing, and storage of a large number of varied purpose aircraft, in particular bombers. In the final analysis, the Air Ministry decided to develop Castle Donnington which initially only had landing facilities and domestic accommodation for bomber crew, the technical support remaining at Wymeswold. However if Castle Donnington had not been selected it is highly possible that the airbase would have been built at Ragdale as it "would likely have been built on a green field site" due to the lack of potential in other geographical regions. Thankfully neither of the Ragdale sites were chosen for development or the history of this beautiful patch of England would have been quite different. After the war the estate acreage dwindled dramatically, so much so that the total estate size at the time of Phyllis' sale was a mere 376 acres in 1955. The same year war rationing ceased.

When Phyllis was selling Ragdale Hall, one of her greatest concerns was to settle everyone in new accommodation, where necessary, before she moved on. She called on local farmer Peter Freckingham to help. On a number of occasions Peter and Phyllis resettled loyal staff in suitable alternative accommodation in the area. One couple and their daughter moved from a farm on the estate to Yew Tree Farm at Holwell. There were many staff who had worked with the Cantrell-Hubberstys for many years. For example, Jean Todd had been housekeeper and personal maid for more than 40 years before she died while still in service. The relationship had been very strong and Phyllis looked on Jean as a close friend and confidant. Jean's death was a tremendous blow to Phyllis. As in former years, it was the younger parlour maid Edith Bullock and cook Mrs. McKerron, now widowed, who moved with Phyllis to Peans Wood in Sussex. Luigi Loreire and Mr and Mrs Fred Ward also accompanied the household at this time.

As detailed in Country Life magazine on June 16th 1955, the sale of Ragdale Hall and Estate was described by Knight, Frank, and Rutley as a freehold, residential and agricultural estate of 376 acres, comprising 274 acres of grass and 92 arable. By this time the Hall had mains water, electricity and central heating. The estate came with 5 cottages in hand with mains water, which was even laid on to most fields for the animals and an area of woodland. Mr Ward had certainly seen considerable developments during his years at Ragdale Hall.

Ragdale Hall, 1984

Era of Commercial Change

*Charles and
Olga Keightley*

The Keightleys

The late '50s represented the last private ownership when Mr Charles
Keightley acted spontaneously in 1956 and moved onto the estate as
the first stage of his purchase of Ragdale Hall. He established himself
as a gentleman farmer at Ragdale Hall but it wasn't until February
1958 that the final conveyancing transferred full ownership from
Phyllis Cantrell-Hubbersty to himself and his wife, Olga. The
Keightleys moved their family of five children aged between 6 and 14
years old from Burton Hall, Burton on the Wolds where 130 years
earlier, Caroline Shirley, later Duchess De Sforza Cesarini, had grown

up in the care of Mr. and Mrs. Charles Mundy. A considerable refurbishment programme was required before they could take up occupation of the Hall itself. Due to this the family lived for the first year in the gardener's cottage, which stands beside the current entrance barrier, while refurbishment was being carried out. Once the refurbishment was completed they moved into the Hall to enjoy country life as gentile hunting farmers, just as the Cantrell-Hubbersty's had done. The Keightleys had not intended to move again. It was the last time the Hall was used as a private family home.

The Keightley family with their five children, Fiona then 14, Ann 12, Helen 10, Julia 8 and Randall 6, had a successful agricultural machinery business in Loughborough, at what is now the Woolworths building and were therefore in the fortunate position to have the resources to support this large house. Mr. and Mrs. Keightley were also following in the Hall's historical past.

As hunting enthusiasts, Ragdale Hall gave them a prime hunting seat located in the Monday Quorn country. Ragdale Hall estate was a very busy farm as well as a country seat. The working farm produced a lot of wheat but in Mr. Keightley's early days there was no grain dryer

Three of the Keightley family on horseback. L-R Anne, Charles, and Fiona.

at the farm. Until they could build a dryer the grain had to be stored in the only large space in the Hall, the ballroom. Fiona Keightley still remembers the beautiful ballroom with its enormous mirrors and pictures on the walls and lovely furniture.

When the grain was stored in the ballroom Mr. Keightley was insistent that the beautiful wooden dance floor be protected as much as possible from the unusual purpose to which the room was being used. When the time came for the removal of the grain from the room the workmen had to cover their shovels in material so that they did not damage the flooring. Part of the refurbishment at this time included the erection of three large 16-foot high silos, built along the original servant's wing of the house, which could store all the future grain crops. When the new grain dryer had been built and all the grain had been removed from the ballroom, the children remember helping to restore the ballroom floor to its former glory. They were encouraged to run about and dance on the floor all day with dusters covering their shoes to which polish had been applied. It was a terrifically fun time for them and a happy time for the whole family.

Life at Ragdale Hall during holiday time was very exciting for the five children. During the school terms the children went to various schools in Derbyshire and Leicestershire so it was in the summer months that they ventured into the grounds of the Hall. The children made their own fun by exploring the vast gardens and finding secret paths which were completely overgrown that led them to other concealed parts of the garden. This gave them great delight and many summer holiday adventures.

Mrs. Keightley's talents were much and varied. She was a keen livestock breeder and would show her animals at the local shows. In the few years between 1956 and 1959 Mrs. Keightley filled the old stables with her horses, used for hunting and breeding. She also bred Jersey cows. She loved the garden. The walled garden at the back of the house produced roses, which grew along the walls, and flowers from the green house filled the house. Fruit was grown for both family and staff. She was a great cook and loved baking, creating a warm homely atmosphere much adored by the children. Nursing was also one of her skills and she would tend to the sickly piglets or lambs that the farm hands did not have time to look after. Fiona remembers feeding little piglets in the old kitchen with a bottle feeder and then wrapping the animals in a towel so that they could be put into the aga to be kept warm.

It is not certain if Ragdale Hall ever had a ghost but Fiona remembers spending evenings on her own when her sisters and brother were at school. During these times she would do her homework in a small room just across the corridor from the old kitchen. Fiona remembers feeling very frightened when at times the room would become very cold for no apparent reason and she felt as if someone was watching her.

Like her predecessor, Mrs. Keightley re-opened All Saints Church to the great delight of the villagers of Ragdale. The church has continued to be a supportive presence in the life of the small community ever since.

In the early days of ownership, Mr. Keightley bought up several pockets of land which adjoined the Ragdale Estate expanding the overall acreage again to nearly 1000 acres by the time the Hall was sold in 1959. It was during these early years that Randall Keightley, then 6 years old, remembers his parents buying a small motorised car for him. He really loved it, even to the point of remembering the little car's number plate - FRC 6. Randall was fascinated by mechanised toys, especially an electric train set which was set up by the base of the main staircase in the front Hall. However Randall remembered another car, a large green American Chevrolet, which belonged to a certain Mr. Froggatt who kept returning to the Hall.

Mr. Froggatt approached Mr. and Mrs. Keightley on behalf of himself and his partner, Mr. Robert Chatham, and was determined to acquire the Hall and land for his own commercial endeavours. Several times he approached the Keightley's before his offer was sufficient to make it prudent for them to accept. The Hall was finally sold in December 1959 to Messers Froggatt and Chatham. Overnight Ragdale Hall became a commercial concern for the first time in its history. It was to be many years before it was privately owned again. The Keightley family moved to Wartnaby Castle, which the children called "Little Belvoir" and interestingly they also took with them the large green American Chevy, so admired by Randall. The Chevy had been thrown in with the deal.

Ragdale Hall Country Club
Froggatt-Chatham Partnership

With this purchase the Hall ceased to be a private house, marking the end of a 175 year hunting era that had commenced with the Earl Ferrers and finished, rather abruptly, when the Keightley family sold to the Froggatt and Chatham Partnership. The purchase in December 1959 was made in two clear lots. Mr. Froggatt bought the land while Mr. Chatham bought the Hall. The Hall stood alone high on the hill for all to see as clearly as it had in the days when it had been the

Robert Chatham

epicentre of a vast hunting estate. Times had changed dramatically for the Hall but although no longer a private residence, this was not the end of this historic story. Following the purchase Mr. Robert and Mrs. Fay Chatham moved their "Old Park Farm Country Club" business from Six Hills to Ragdale Hall in January 1960. During their time at the Hall they succeeded in drawing a wide membership from around the area and many visitors from all over the world stayed at the Ragdale Hall Country Club. Mr and Mrs Chatham's clients could avail themselves of a series of pastimes and some took the opportunity of joining the Quorn Hunt during their stay.

Robert Chatham owned and managed the Hall with his wife and along with other commercial developments at the Hall they started a small games room located in the tower with a Black Jack table and Roulette wheel. The room was originally set up using a professional croupier. It appears that this croupier had connections with the well known Kray twins. It is rumoured that on at least one occasion the Kray twins visited the Hall during this period. A cavalcade of large black limousines is remembered arriving at the front door of the Hall carrying some very important passengers from London.

The Krays at The Kentucky Club, East London. From left, Reggie, Ray, Uncle Bill, Charlie (father), Charlie (eldest son) and Ronnie

Robert Chatham got a real shock when this happened, suddenly realising that he was no longer in control of developments in the games room. He was apparently not aware of the connection between the Kray twins and his professional croupier. He became very concerned by the fact that the games room had attracted some rather high profile visitors and he had every right to be extremely apprehensive. This was at a time when the twins were at the height of their notoriety and had begun to expand their affairs outside London into other towns. The Midlands was no exception to their attentions and eventually in 1963 the Kray twins opened a club in Leicester. Together with the help of some of their associates, they were soon carrying out activities along the same lines as they had in London. Knowledge of their visits to Ragdale Hall spread into the community quite quickly. Tentative police enquiries were made into the general activities at Ragdale Hall together with the rumoured visits of the twins. However it would appear that the incidents remained rather low key, not attracting official intervention, but the Kray twins visits to the Hall remain much remembered in the community today.

Perhaps fortunately for Robert Chatham the partnership did not last more than a few years before the business went into liquidation in March 1963. It is possible that the high price paid for the estate by Mr. Froggatt, played a part in the eventual short-lived Froggatt and Chatham Partnership. At this time Mr. and Mrs. Chatham closed the Ragdale Hall Country Club and started a business in The Olde Stocks Restaurant, Grimston, where they continued for some years. Mr. Froggatt sold the land to Mr. Edward Carleton Richardson of Home Farm, Ragdale Village.

Ragdale Hall Country Club
Thomas Edward Boynton

After a six months closure period Mr. Thomas Edward Boynton purchased the Hall in October 1963 when he was 61 years of age "more as a hobby than anything else" says his daughter Pat, "following the guidance and encouragement of his Bank Manager". Thomas Boynton was a Yorkshire-born research and development engineer whose companies included Ratby Engineering Company Ltd, which he founded after the war in 1947 and eventually sold to Lindustries many years later. He was an entrepreneur and an avid inventor. Challenging himself he bought his own airplane and learned to fly when he was 50 years old. Another project he got involved in arose from his acquaintance with the originator of the car window, registration number etching system, for car security. Unfortunately he could not get anyone in the car manufacturing industry interested in that idea at the time. It wasn't until many years later that this system came on to the market. Indeed the system has proved to be so successful that nowadays there is hardly a car on the road without their car number etched on to their windows.

The Hall was sold to Mr. Boynton for £17,500. Following the liquidation of the previous partnership the bank was holding the Hall as collateral and it was having considerable difficulty selling the property. To put the final purchase price in context, a local family

Thomas
Edward Boynton

house in the area would have sold for approximately £1000 at the time. At the point of purchase the Hall had been vacant for six months from March 1963 to October 1963. Mr. Boynton's daughter Pat recalls the first day that she and her family came up to see the Hall for the first time following her father's purchase.

"That day the front door was unlocked and the Hall was completely deserted. We went into the Hall and looked around, everything was spotlessly clean as if the owners had just stepped out for a moment. It was a beautiful sunny day and the windows were open to let in fresh air. There were vases of fresh flowers everywhere. We went up stairs and moved from room to room trying to find someone, everything was

John and Judy
Maddaford's
wedding party at
the back of the
Hall: John Gordon
Anne Gordon,
Gladys Maddaford,
Stella Whittingham,
Barnie Tonkinson,
John Maddaford,
Judy Maddaford,
Helen Knox,
Joy Christie,
Barbara and Bill
Morrison

so spick and span, but there was no one to be found. We were just preparing to leave when we saw some one in the garden and found out that this couple were the only two people left at the Hall. They had been faithfully caring for the Hall until the new owners arrived."

Pat says her mother was not initially impressed by her husband buying the Hall as she did not wish to live there and she continued to live at the family home in Leicester. The family does admit however that owning the Hall was a very happy experience for them. Her father continued to run the Hall as a Country Club until 1969. He re-opened it as a private members' club, circulating all the previous members, informing them about the new ownership and nudged the membership up to 700. He also encouraged the visitors to the Quorn and the Belvoir hunts to stay at the Hall whilst hunting in the area. The residential facilities comprised 14 centrally heated bedrooms, each fitted with a shower only and a telephone. Each room was named after a famous hunt. The dining facilities were located in the old ballroom and could accommodate 150 people seated, or 200 for a buffet. This ability to accommodate large numbers of people allowed Thomas Boynton to promote the Hall as an ideal reception venue.

In May 1964 Thomas Boynton purchased just under three acres of land from Mr. Edward Richardson of Home Farm, Ragdale. This particular piece of land at the back of the Hall ensured uninterrupted access to all sides of the Hall for vehicles and allowed free flow of traffic around the Hall for the first time in some years. This all round access was to become most important for subsequent owners.

The grounds were much more wooded at that time in keeping with many Hall's of a similar nature. The quarter-mile long drive ran through a beautiful little wood which surrounded the Hall on three sides, planted with beech, oak, elm and silver birch and the gardens to the back of the house were walled, enclosing flowering shrubs, fruit trees and, believe it or not, peach houses.

Mrs. Cuthbertson, a Scottish lady, living in the flat at the top of the house which Nanny Irving used to occupy, was Mr. Boynton's business manager. She policed the staff, ensuring that the Hall did not suffer any fraudulent activity or theft of items such as foodstuffs, drink and even cash, which had happened in former times. In those days a lot of the staff lived in at the Hall and Mrs. Cuthbertson also managed the staff's residential arrangements. She proved herself to be both loyal to her employers and efficient at her job right up until the Hall was sold.

Mr. Boynton had a Spanish headwaiter called Carlos. Carlos was in charge of the dining room arrangements and his girlfriend Angela managed reception. They were both very popular with the customers and they stayed at Ragdale Hall for most of the Boynton ownership. In the '60s the gaming laws were relaxed sufficiently to allow Mr. Boynton to re-open the Roulette and Blackjack tables in a gaming room now located in what had been Phyllis Cantrell-Hubbersty's old flower room and is today the main reception area. With Carlos acting as croupier, the gaming room opened after the dining room closed in the evening. Together with the private bar, guests were encouraged to play until the early hours.

Outside a kidney shaped heated swimming pool, measuring 55 feet by 20 feet, had been built together with poolside facilities, following a customer care questionnaire asking the members of the club for their ideas and suggestions. The pool was top of their list of requests.

Photographs of this period show that four small towers positioned at roof level on the front elevation had already been removed before the Boynton family purchase. After 6 years ownership aged 69 years Mr. Boynton sold the Hall to Mr. Demetrios Kaouklis for £34,000 (just over £400,000 in today's money) and doubling his money.

Ragdale Hall Hotel Ltd

The Hall was sold to Mr. Demetrios Kaouklis with the understanding that he and his family would actually live at the Hall. Demetrios Kaouklis was a Greek gentleman who owned the Copper Kettle restaurant in Melton Mowbray at the time of purchasing Ragdale Hall. Initially he opened the Hall as a hotel with a restaurant and club. In March 1970 he had a new wing added to accommodate new conference and banqueting facilities. The intention was to create a conference centre for the Midlands, specialising in the training of industrial and technical sales representatives. The new wing cost £23,000 (just under £245,000 today) and created a further 12 bedrooms. The project never really developed into a success and unfortunately he only held on to the concern for a couple of years before going into liquidation.

The venture had not gone well for some time because when the Hall transferred ownership to Tom Eyton of Slimming Magazine in 1971 Audrey Eyton described the Hall as in a "state of disrepair with the gardens overgrown and in great need of attention".

Slimming Magazine

Slimming Magazine was founded in 1970 by Mr Tom Eyton, and the organisation bought Ragdale Hall in 1971 when they decided to diversify into Slimming Clubs. Ragdale Hall became the head office and main club for the organisation. The Hall provided the perfect central geographical base for Slimming Clubs, as the Slimming Magazine and Slimming Clubs concept had been particularly successful in Leicestershire and the Midlands. The Hall acted as a perfect rendezvous for clients attending residential slimming weeks and for the Slimming Club Leaders' annual meetings. A refurbishment programme started immediately to bring the Hall to a high residential standard which would reflect that expected of a top UK health hydro. It took the Eytons two years to achieve this.

In February 1973 the Quorn Hunt made a rare appearance, meeting at Ragdale Hall for the first time in many years. The Master of Foxhounds was Mrs. Ulrica Murray Smith who had already held the mastership for 13 years and was to continue in the post for a further 12 years, totalling 25 years in all, making her service the longest individual mastership of the century. During her time, she became one of the most popular women in the county. It was also during these years that the original Ragdale estate acres were sold again in 1974 to the Bowley family who continue to farm the surrounding land to this present time.

The health hydro concept was really beginning to develop at Ragdale Hall. The prime source of clientele still came from the slimming clubs' national network. There were 527 clubs in existence at the time and 400 ladies who ran them. The throughput of slimmers was enormous. A slimmer would attend their local slimming club for an average of only 8 to 10 weeks during which time the Hall was promoted to the group. So every 10 weeks there was a complete changeover of potential clientele for the health hydro. The incentive for the club leaders to promote Ragdale Hall was that they would qualify for a free stay at the health hydro for every 6 guests they sent along. Needless to say the leaders loved to stay at Ragdale and the competition between them to be recognised as the top national club leader was fierce. The clients would then subscribe to the bi-monthly Slimming Magazine and a percentage of these clients would progress to become regular health hydro clients. In those early hydro years, the business system was simple and resulted in almost 50% of Ragdale's clientele coming from the slimming clubs. An average stay was 3.2 to 3.8 days, rising to 4.2 days per stay in the autumn months

At this stage in health hydro history the market was very underdeveloped. The public impression was that "health farms" were an expensive pastime for rich people who wanted to lose weight over a short period of time using fairly drastic measures. Encouraged by the changing needs in society to provide this type of service, Ragdale Hall Health Hydro was now developing well. It had a sauna, massage rooms and a growing beauty salon and the cost of a week's stay in one of its 25 bedrooms was between £65 and £70 per person.

Slimming Magazine was also thriving. By 1973 its bi-monthly publication had a national circulation of 147,780. By today's standards that figure was extremely good compared with the current circulation figure for the second largest slimming magazine in todays more developed marketplace, 'Rosemary Conley Diet and Fitness', which has a circulation of 151,705. Slimming Magazine had comparable figures 30 years ago. The requirement for slimming publications has also risen over the years as is reflected in the current largest slimming publication 'Slimming World' with a circulation figure at a resounding 255,726 and a target audience comprising "aspiring women aged between 25 to 44 years of age".

The major focus of a health hydro in those days was the slimming requirement. People did not worry about stress levels then - that phenomenon was still in the future.

Audrey Eyton, dietitian and author of the book "The F Plan Diet", joined her husband Tom at the health hydro in 1974 promoting well-being through a healthy and balanced diet. Initially Audrey fulfilled the dietitian role within the Hall for all the clients but, as the Hall got busier, she handed this over to another dietitian and she remained as a consultant.

Audrey is described by staff members who remember her, as being a lovely person to work along side, accommodating and gentle, with an ability to get along very well with everyone. Unfortunately the same cannot be said for her husband Tom who apparently had a particularly caustic managerial style. He had a reputation for being an aggressive manager with the ability to sack staff, not only on the spot, but also in their absence while on their day off. He could be really ruthless. It is reported that on one occasion he sacked the entire housekeeping team, while on another occasion he sacked the garden staff because they missed a section of lawn when mowing. It is said that each year when the top national Slimming Club Leader was to be presented with her trophy and her holiday trip, Tom would have the winner weighed and if she did not weigh within the correct range for her height and build, the trophy or the reward trip was not awarded to her. Consequently all the staff were afraid of him. The clients however loved him, he had their interests at heart and in his own way he got things done.

Carl Wilson however, has his own story to tell. He drove for Tom Eyton in the '70s and says that he was not as bad as he was painted. Tom owned a beautiful burgundy Bentley with tan leather upholstery and, acting as chauffeur, Carl often drove Tom and Audrey to the Quorn Country Club or other similar establishment for the evening. He would then pick them up in the early hours of the morning, even though he had to get up for work at 5:30am. Carl was Tom's transport driver and was obviously well respected by Tom Eyton for his reliability. Tom could be generous to those who really performed for him. On one occasion he asked Carl if he would be his fulltime personal chauffeur, but Carl declined as he felt it was best to keep arrangements as they were.

The focus of Ragdale as a Health Hydro, in the early days under the auspices of the Eyton's, was to help clients lose weight during their stay and to act as a guide towards a permanent solution of weight control when they had returned home. Audrey had carried out some dietary research and been involved in advising Slimming Club clients on weight loss while they were still eating 1000 calories per day. Some people would arrive at the health hydro totally convinced that they were beyond help and that they couldn't lose weight even if they did only consume 1000 calories a day. Audrey Eyton worked with these people by putting them on a diet of 1500 calories per day, while they believed they were on less and as a result they still lost weight. Some of this research material from programmes carried out at Ragdale Hall went into the compilation of her book, "The F Plan Diet".

Under the guidance of Audrey the daily regime for clients at the Hall started without breakfast - unless they particularly requested breakfast, and therefore paid for as an extra expense. Most clients were on either a 750 or a 500 calorie-a-day diet and they would swim or exercise, have a massage or a beauty treatment in the morning conducted by one of only 17 therapists in the beauty department at that time. This was followed by a buffet lunch served in the dining room. By lunch time they were ravenous, so queuing for lunch was commonplace to ensure an early sitting.

Dinner was the main meal of the day and reflected some of the former grandeur of the Hall. Silver service was provided and full dinner dress was required of all guests. Diners sat at large refectory tables and feasted on a typical choice of:-

Dinner Menu
Prawn Cocktail
Grilled Cinnamon Grapefruit
A Choice of Citrus Fruits

Steamed Fish
Grilled Dover Sole
Grilled Plaice

Three Vegetables (no carbohydrates)

Tea or Coffee or Iced Lemon water

Behind the scenes, kitchen staff started their duty day at 8am and most meals were prepared during the day for about 50 guests. The kitchen ran a split shift system so that two meals could be provided using the same kitchen team. Olive Goodacre, who was the only cook at that time, coped with an overall 14-hour day with a few hours off in the middle of the afternoon. Today the kitchen is staffed with 15 fulltime chefs, preparing all the choices on the menu and working in shifts to provide the guests with top quality cuisine. In the '70s all foods had to be easy to prepare but there was one added extra to the evening meal which could be ordered in advance. A fresh trout from Ragdale's moat, caught that day, was served for the guests that evening. All drinks were of the Schweppes slimline variety except iced lemon water which was made in the Hall's kitchen by the gallon. It was free and it was very popular with the guests, especially after their saunas and exercise classes. In case of emergencies there was a hostelry close at hand if the meals' regime became too much for some guests. They could slip along to the 'Six Hills Hotel', then known as the 'Durham Ox' and order a "normal meal" for a quick shot of higher calories. Consequently for most guests a week's weight loss could be around 5 to 6lbs.

The Hall's top quota was 50 guests and so it was a much more subdued place to visit compared to today. During the '70s there was one general manager, Chris Boardman who with his deputy, Peter Godfrey managed the four heads of department. These were head of gardening, head of driving, head of beauty and head of dining room. As a business, Ragdale Hall would close for Christmas in the '70s from December 17th to January 2nd. This more relaxed approach finally stopped some years later when it was bought by Leisure Developments. In October 1979, just before the Eyton's sold their Slimming Magazine business which included Ragdale Hall, Martin Wooton was appointed Ragdale's Hotel Manager. He worked with the Eyton's for six months before the Hall was sold as part of the Slimming Magazine and Clubs business to S.M. Leisure. Martin was to remain with the Hall as general manager for the next ten years encompassing a few ownership changes during that developmental period.

Argos Press Group – S.M.Leisure

The Eyton's sold their Slimming Magazine and Slimming Clubs business for 3.8 million pounds to the BET Group. Mr. Richard Quinlan bought the business through the BET subsidiary Argos Press Group and continued the Ragdale Hall Health Hydro business under the canopy of S.M.Leisure, which was itself a wholly owned subsidiary of the Argos Press Group.

Mr. Quinlan invested heavily in the business, spending £500,000 on a conversion and updating programme. This included an extension of the 60-seater dining room in 1980 into what had been the library, allowing seating for another 30 guests, nudging the concern towards a top class luxury establishment. Interestingly Argos Press didn't actually want Ragdale Hall as they normally didn't involve themselves with freehold properties and had taken steps to sell off all existing freehold properties in their portfolio. They only wanted the Slimming

Magazine and Slimming Clubs business, but in order to acquire these they had to include the purchase of the Hall. In particular, the Slimming Clubs were very profitable and they did not require any further capital outlay.

At this stage the existing management team decided to attempt a management buy out and investigated the possibilities. The Hall was acquirable for about £100,000. However they were dissuaded at that time by Nicholas Wills, one of the BET Vice Chairmen, who argued that the Hall had no future and that they would be better to go and

Richard Quinlan

work for Trusthouse Forte. It was at this point that Nicholas Wills came in to see the Hall and declared that he thought they were all "bloody mad" in planning to buy it. In fleeing the place never to return his parting comment was "do what you can with the place and we will sell it as soon as we can". Armed with this restrictive remit the management team decided to try to look favourably at the Hall and make this health hydro work like a proper business. Martin Wooton, General Manager at this time felt, that the business could only work if it was a really first-class establishment.

There was a mixture of staff skills, some were very good and some were not so good. Coralie Wodham was appointed head of beauty and she did a superb job laying the building blocks for what was to

115

become recognised as one of the best beauty departments in the U.K. In the early days, management had daily lunchtime meetings to keep abreast of the changes being implemented and the impact these were having on the company. The perceived forerunner in the U.K. health hydro market at the time was Champneys. So after a couple of months of Ragdale's ownership by S.M. Leisure, it was agreed that the only way to be really successful in the health hydro market was to challenge Champneys head on.

"Lets enjoy it," said Martin, "There is no other way."

He researched the facilities provided by other UK health hydros for their guests, the commercial awareness of staff and how they applied this in their dealings with guests. Martin says that some of these principles and methodologies were applied to Ragdale Hall.

The marketing approach had to be designed to achieve positive promotional progress to reach the potential new client with this exciting news of change at the Hall. Glossy magazines were encouraged to cover the Hall in promotional articles to assist in the raising of the Hall's profile in its specific target marketplace. Newspapers also played their part with local and national papers promoting the Hall and its changes to the general public at large.

As a consequence when Champneys was sold to Earnest Saunders of the Guinness Group, his wife came to Ragdale Hall to establish why Ragdale Hall was doing three times the amount of treatments that Champneys was doing at that time. Martin put this down to a considerable in-house promotion campaign, which was coupled with real personal interest in the guests. All the staff at Ragdale Hall were trained to act as a team in relation to the guest so that the whole service appeared to be seamless. Also the guests would be toured around the Hall and shown how to get the best out of their stay for themselves. This personal attention assisted the guests to become more familiar with the Hall and its workings.

Martin also got some help from his friends at Marks and Spencer, who were experts in the psychology of the guest. He wanted to change the custom of men dressing in black tie for dinner and women wearing lots of with jewellery. Marks and Spencer's told him to equalise all guests as Ragdale Hall guests by introducing a relaxed culture where everyone dressed at all times in their Ragdale Hall dressing gowns or the Ragdale Hall track suits, produced specifically for this purpose. This levelling approach, rather like that of the school uniform, worked very well for all the guests who found their stay at the Hall more relaxing. To support this the management team produced a brochure called "The Quiet Revolution" in which it stated on almost every page that guests should wear a housecoat or tracksuit at all times. Today most health hydros apply this approach.

The central geographical location of the Hall was convenient for new guests from all four corners of the country. Although the Slimming Club client continued to come to Ragdale Hall, whole sections of society were not being catered for in the health hydro business. Ragdale decided to change all that and position itself to attract a wideband of general public, some who had never even dreamed of going to a health hydro before. There were two distinct types of guest now at Ragdale Hall - one was the seasoned, wealthy health hydro veteran who often stayed for a week and the other was the first timer guest from the Slimming Clubs who mainly stayed for a two-day health hydro taster. Those carrying out the Hall's marketing pushed these two-day tasters hard. Marketing however still remained a problem, as marketing expertise, as such, did not exist amongst the staff. In the first year after BET bought the Hall the business turned over £170,000 and at times had a maximum occupancy of only 40%. With focused effort the occupancy grew quite quickly to 65-70%, but to get it above that was proving to be a struggle. Following these first efforts, which produced a small profit, BET got out as quickly as they could, selling the Hall to Leisure Investments for £1 million. Ten times the amount it would have sold for in 1980.

Leisure Investments plc

Having bought the Hall alone for £1 million in July 1984, Leisure Investments pledged to spend a further £350,000 on the establishment. With Mr. Robert Upsdell, Chief Executive, the building programme was to include the installation of an essential new indoor swimming pool and the refurbishment of the existing bedrooms. This would include rewiring, painting, decorating and finishing off a development project in the kitchen that had been started by the Eyton's but never finished. Half the floor area was apparently still just soil flooring and there was no damp proof course in the newly built kitchen areas.

The building of the indoor swimming pool was started in December 1983 and opened a few months later in May 1984 at a cost of £236,400. Having an indoor swimming pool put Ragdale Hall in the big players' league which is where they had planned to be. The company also planned to introduce a wider selection of health and beauty treatments.

A lack of marketing expertise continued to dog the venture and it was at this time that Philip Rodgers, Marketing Director of Vidal

Sassoon came to visit the Hall with Vidal. He recognised the marketing deficiency and spoke to Martin Wooton who, although embarrassed about the issue, confirmed that marketing needed some help. Philip Rodgers asked about the kind of future market the Hall was planning to attract. Martin informed him that it was the four star market, 75% female 25% male, concentrating on the pampering and spoiling rather than slimming environment. Philip agreed that this was sound thinking and, on return to London, sent Martin a copy of Cosmopolitan Magazine saying, "Just do as you are told and we will get this place rolling". He put Martin in touch with his public relations officer, Penny Ryder and Nicky Lyons-Maris who was Marketing Director for Cosmopolitan Magazine. Together they agreed a deal at a much-reduced price with the magazine for a "two guests for the price of one" promotion which was advertised as a two-page spread in the April 1984 edition. At the Hall, the new wing which had only held one bed per room since 1970, was being upgraded by the introduction of a second bed into each room to suit this offer. Ragdale management thought that the Cosmopolitan promotion would result in about half a dozen rooms being filled for a few weeks. To their amazement the response was colossal and it filled every room in the Hall for the next 18 months. This, together with Vidal Sassoon's fashion orientated advice that the Hall should keep up with the changing exercise and treatment fashion trends, meant that the hydro managed to gain momentum ahead of the competition and develop a leading edge in health hydro trend setting.

Subsequently Ragdale management went on to do deals with other journals such as Good Housekeeping and Woman's Journal. Although the responses were good, they were never as massive as the original run with Cosmopolitan. Ragdale's management had identified the advantage of having a full quota of guests in the Hall as the extra per-capita spend attached to that was high. The Hall had a brand new indoor pool, refurbished outdoor pool with additional changing rooms and its bedrooms were filled with guests. Business life at Ragdale had changed for the better. At last Ragdale Hall Health Hydro was on its way.

Mr. Upsdell became Chairman of a newly formed company Health and Leisure Holdings and Mr. John Knight also joined him from Leisure Developments as Financial Director on the board. This new company was set up to operate Ragdale Hall as a health hydro and to develop the business into further health related investment areas. The cost of a stay at Ragdale had reduced from the Slimming Magazine days to "£50.00 per night all in". This maximised market attractiveness

Evening at Ragdale Hall

119

A hunting map of the region from 1865

120

The Old Hall as seen from the village

123

Ragdale Hall and grounds in 1964

The view from the roof

The Keightley children Anne, Helen, Randall, Julie and Fiona

Dining as in 'Slimming Magazine' days

One of two suites with spiral staircases built in the '80s

The Terrace Suite as it was in the '70s

Above and facing page, the old stables

Facing page and left,
excavations behind the Hall

A selection of promotional materials from the '70s and '80s and right, Audrey Eyton's best-selling 'F-Plan Diet'

Show someone you **really** care this Christmas

A Ragdale Hall gift voucher is the perfect Christmas gift – an opportunity to be pampered in the truly relaxing and luxurious surroundings of one of Britain's leading health resorts.

Day packages start at £79 and overnight stays from £87, both offering a sumptuous choice of health and beauty treatments, fitness activities and full use of the extensive facilities.

It is just so easy ... vouchers are available for day visits or residential stays or in monetary values from £25.

Vouchers are valid for one year from the date of purchase and are sent in a wallet with a brochure which is presented in an attractive gift pack!

Vouchers are dispatched upon receipt of payment.

Cheques should be made payable to Ragdale Hall. For immediate dispatch you may telephone quoting your credit card number. We accept Visa, Access, American Express and Switch. Alternatively, you may visit our website at www.ragdalehall.co.uk and order your vouchers on line.

Spoil someone special this year with a Ragdale Hall Gift Voucher

---

Ragdale Hall voted Health Spa of the Year 1999

At a glittering Oscars type ceremony at London's Intercontinental Hotel, Ragdale were recently presented with the coveted Health Spa of the Year 1999 Award.

The awards themselves were run by Professional Beauty Magazine and sponsored by Good Housekeeping. What most delighted us was that all votes were cast by our guests! Once we were nominated, we were then judged anonymously by three separate independent judges just to make sure that our guests were telling the truth!

Professional Beauty Magazine said "The customer definitely comes first at Ragdale and this is why so many of them voted. This, coupled with Ragdale's continuing professional development meant that the judging panel agreed – Ragdale Hall is the Best Health Spa 1999".

We are all extremely proud to have received the award, but it only makes us more determined to continue endeavouring to improve both our service and of course our facilities. We sincerely thank all the guest's who took the time to vote for us.

Incidentally, two of our therapists - Keeley Beck-Smith and Everton Greaves reached the finals of the Therapist of the Year too!

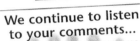

We continue to listen to your comments…

For a while now, guests have been commenting that despite their affection for the historical atmosphere of the old part of the Hall, the dark panelling especially in the dining room, was rather too sombre and dreary and not perhaps now inkeeping with the airy, relaxed luxury of the rest of the Hall and the style of cuisine now being enjoyed.

Our plans to completely refurbish the dining room (which has now

new lease of life for the next two hundred years!

By early in the New Year, we hope to show you a dining room that reflects the original style of our lovely old house and also offers an atmosphere of relaxed luxury that only Ragdale can create. There will also be a whole new layout with a wider selection of tables for all sizes of parties from twos upwards!

Our refurbishment of bedrooms continues as well and during the autumn two of our suites, the Shares and the Wolds will get a totally new

---

the future and beyond

By the summer Ragdale will be opening the doors on our superb new fitness area which will include a 2000ft² state of the art new gymnasium plus two new exercise studios.

The gym will feature the very latest pieces of equipment in separate zones for cardiovascular work and a free weight section and will include a cardio theatre facility with personal headphones.

The opening of our two new exercise studios will herald

using visualisation to provide a virtual mind trip on wheels. It's suitable for everyone, after all, it's as easy as riding a bike!

Dance classes have always been a favourite here at the Hall, so now we are offering an even greater choice. On your next visit you can look forward to disco, salsa and funk, ensuring you'll be the centre of attention at your next Christmas party!

Our real pioneering work however is in the field of mind/body where a plethora of new and in some cases unique sessions, will help you achieve ultimate fitness through mental strength leading to excellent physical improvements Look out for Chi Gung, Chinese Wand, Pilates and Fusion, not to mention candlelit relaxation.

The Ragdale Hall Newsletter Spring/Summer 1999

Major refurbishment now all finished!

In January, we completed the final stage of our major programme of refurbishments and improvements that have been ongoing for three years. **We can now boast the finest, most up to date and most spacious facilities of any health spa in the UK.**

It all started in October 1998 when we opened the new Swimming Pool, Spa Complex and refurbished and requipped the Exercise Pool. This was followed in August 1999 with the new fitness areas (two studios and gymnasium) and our acclaimed new programme of classes and activities, followed in March 2000 and finally……and we are still getting our breath back!……the final piece of the jigsaw in January 2001. Details of this lovely new building are overleaf.

It's now all here for you to enjoy - so come and be pampered, relax and rejuvenate, and then……

tell us how we can improve Ragdale even more!!

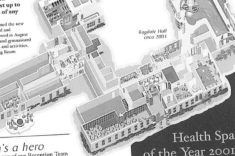

Ragdale Hall circa 2001

SPRING NEWSLETTER 2001

Ragdale Hall HEALTH HYDRO

Hearn's a hero

Paul Hearn, one of our Reception Team recently won the highly prized title Employee of the Year for 2000.

Many guests will remember Paul when he started at Ragdale nearly two years ago as a Porter, working alongside his step father Roger.

As well as transferring to Reception last year, he has also helped out as a relief Night Porter and by driving the staff minibus - in is, in fact, Paul's flexibility and willingness that first made him stand out from the crowd.

His real star quality, however, is his gentle and cheerful manner when dealing with both colleagues and guests alike and his genuine desire to help. Paul was presented with a Calvin Klein watch and certificate and commented "It was rather a shock but I was very honoured. Working at Ragdale is all about people and that's what I love about the job most. Seeing guests arrive from a stressful journey, helping them settle in and seeing them the next day relaxed and glowing, gives me a real buzz".

A STAR!

behind-the-scenes Maintenance Team, who showed exceptional qualities of loyalty, conscientiousness and above all, good humour with colleagues and guests alike.

When asked why he liked working at Ragdale he replied "The girls …… and the friendly working environment!!".

Managing Director, David Harndorff, presenting Steve with his certificate and watch.

Health Spa of the Year 2001

Having won the title for the last two years, we were excited but nonetheless a little taken aback to be informed that we were yet again finalists for the 2001 title. We sincerely thank all guests who voted for us and are currently nervously awaiting the judge's decision.

Promotional newsletters from 1999 and 2001

The indoor pool built in 1984

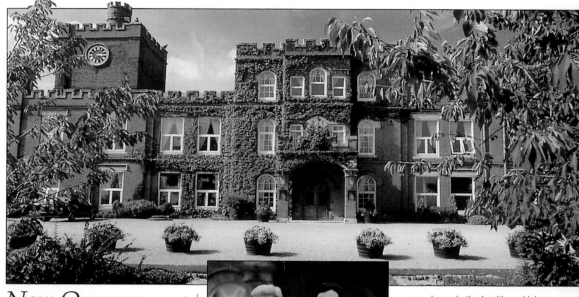

New Owners Retain Old Style

At Ragdale Hall we're very proud of our reputation as one of the foremost health hydros in the country and under our new owners we hope you'll think it's even better than before.

Garry Nesbitt and Michael Isaacs purchased the hall last June. Formerly owners of Our Price Records, which they sold to W. H. Smith, both were keen to move into the leisure industry. They are highly enthusiastic about Ragdale Hall and are learning the business rapidly. They are about to complete a refurbishment and expansion programme with the aim of offering you some of the very best health and fitness facilities you'll find anywhere in the whole of Europe.

Garry Nesbitt comments:

"The hall may have new owners but it still very much retains its former friendliness. No one is ever daunted by its grandeur and everyone is made very welcome and encouraged to feel at home."

Garry was encouraged to buy the hall when it went into receivership (due to its parent company's problems) last year by his wife, Penny, who was a frequent guest at Ragdale. With a strong belief in hands-on ownership Garry and Michael are frequently at the Hall and enjoy chatting to guests. In fact many of you may have met them already.

Familiar Faces

Frequent visitors to the hall will be pleased to know that you'll still find the same familiar faces next time you visit. Jean Oliver is the new managing director and all the former management team are still in place.

Jean, who has been at Ragdale for over nine years, is a well known name in the Beauty industry. Heading a team of over 170 members of staff, many of whom have been at the Hall for many years, Jean and her senior managers have extensive experience in the health and leisure industry.

She prides herself that in Britain, Ragdale leads the way in offering the latest treatments, "We always endeavour to be

first on the market with the very latest techniques," she said, "and once the extension is completed we will be more than a match for any health hydro in this country or in Europe".

Facing, Newsletter from Michael and Garry's 1st year and, this page, celebrating their 5th year at the Hall

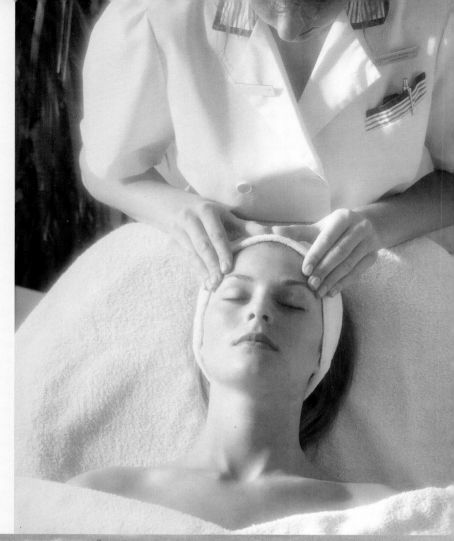

*A beauty therapist
at work*

The Beauty Therapists in 1992

Ragdale Hall's superb cuisine

Aerial shot of the Hall, 1996

The Garden Room

The Verandah

The Gym

The Front Lounge

143

The Studios

Meditation

The Dining Room

Pampurrs

SHOULDER
MASSAGE

The new pool complex

Ragdale Hall

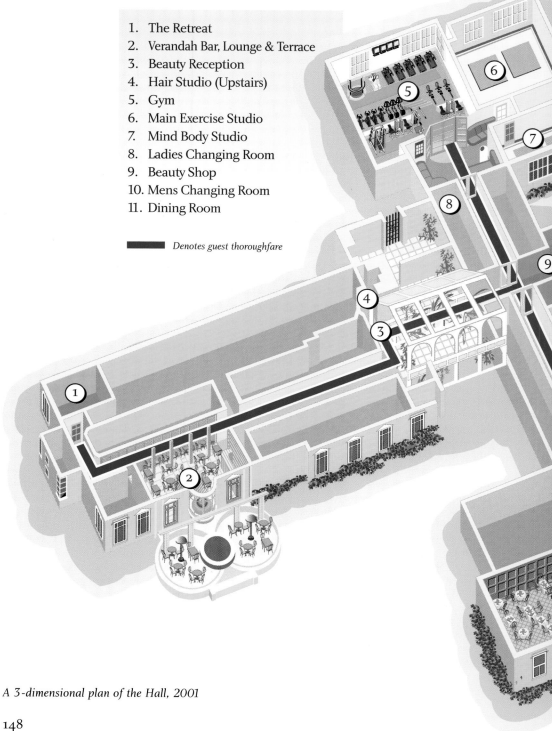

1. The Retreat
2. Verandah Bar, Lounge & Terrace
3. Beauty Reception
4. Hair Studio (Upstairs)
5. Gym
6. Main Exercise Studio
7. Mind Body Studio
8. Ladies Changing Room
9. Beauty Shop
10. Mens Changing Room
11. Dining Room

Denotes guest thoroughfare

A 3-dimensional plan of the Hall, 2001

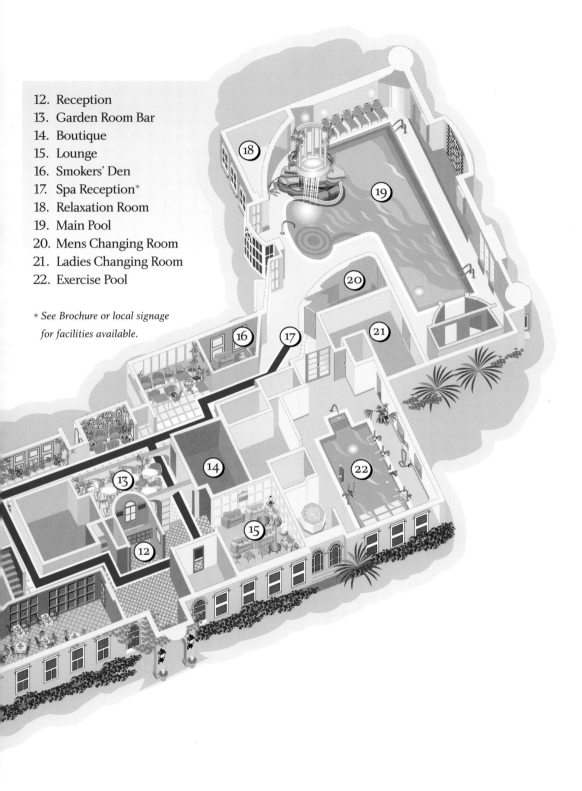

Pippa Woodroffe opens the new dining room extension, April 2000

The 2nd of two consecutive
Professional Beauty Health Spa
of the Year Awards achieved
1999 and 2000

Professional Beauty 2000
Awards
WINNER
BEST HEALTH SPA

in the increasingly competitive marketplace. By this stage the Hall offered 78 different treatments and activities split into four main areas - fitness, slimming, beauty, and relaxation for stress. The guest profile was 80% female, 20% male with approx 40% of these guests making regular return visits. The emphasis was more towards relaxation as opposed to slimming and guests were still encouraged to remain in their dressing gowns or track suits for dinner and not to worry about dressing up in the evening.

It was at this stage in 1984 that Ragdale Hall ventured into recording. It made a long-playing album of exercises and aerobics to encourage its guests to "move to music" at home while remembering all that they had been taught during their stay. The album came with two posters, each representing a side of the LP, illustrating exercises to be adopted as the album progressed through its musical repertoire.

Other ventures were afoot. An attempt was made to develop a horse riding facility from the Ragdale Hall stables at the back of the Hall. A local lady, Helen Harvey, placed a few horses there and Tony Edwards had some of his jousting mares there for a time. A few guests would borrow horses to join the Quorn Hunt but by now this activity was frowned upon and soon not enough guests were taking advantage of the facility of horse riding to make it worthwhile. In 1985,the final year of Ulrica Murray-Smith's mastership of the Quorn, the Boxing Day Hunt met for the last time at Ragdale Hall. As in the previous years of '82 and '83, the hunt was joined by Prince Charles just before moving off. In keeping with the tide of public opinion, it was becoming increasingly unpopular to maintain the association with the hunt. Consequently, the hunt has not been encouraged to meet at Ragdale Hall since that time, signifying the end of an era.

By this stage of development, day guest numbers were beginning to rise as more and more women were taking advantage of the top to toe one-day pamper packages. As a result of this the Hall was getting busier at lunch times, filling the new dining area which had been extended in 1980. There were now three sittings scheduled for guests at lunchtime - 12:30, 1pm, and 1:30pm depending on their personal treatment schedule that day. Operating lunch times this way worked out to be very economical for Ragdale Hall and its kitchen staff.

All the most recently built rooms had their own shower and all the rooms in the Hall had been refurbished in 1983 and 1984 to include ensuite shower rooms or bathrooms. The price of a stay in 1986 varied from £24:00 for a day visit, £50:00 per person per night for a twin room with shower and toilet, £60:00 per person per night for a studio room with bath, shower and toilet, and the ultimate in comfort, a suite

*Ulrica Murray-Smith
cantering up the
drive at Ragdale
Hall, 1985*

at £75:00 per person per night. The Eyton's old flat of five rooms at the top of the house, which had previously been the nursery, was redesigned into four individual bedrooms with luxury ensuite bathrooms. In this way the Hall did not have to introduce a higher price for an extra large suite. In the early days one of the best rooms in the house was room 33. This room with its semi-circular window overlooks the garden at the back of the Hall. It had the best TV, a Finlandia, the only TV in the Hall with the luxury of a remote control. Neither of the existing main suites 51 and 52 were in existence until later in the '80s. Designed by Paul Sutton, it was his idea to make the two suites really special by putting in spiral staircases. These remained in the suites until the year 2000 when the suites were refurbished and full staircases replaced the spiral stairs which could be difficult to climb when carrying luggage.

The daily activity list in the mid '80s was a lot less expansive than it is today and sometimes there was a fear that guests may become bored. So as many staff as possible got involved in supporting the various exercise activities introduced to keep guests occupied. A lot of

*Ulrica speaking
to Martin Wooton,
1985*

new exercise classes were introduced including classes held in the evenings. Cookery demonstrations of various Ragdale Hall dishes were very popular and gave the guest culinary ideas they could take home with them. Talks on a variety of health related subjects were also given. Early morning jogging or walking around the surrounding countryside was key for those trying to lose weight. This was often followed by an exercise in the pool or on the outward-bound circuit, set up around the Hall, which included swinging across the moat. Hardest work of all was the back-to-back slimming club weekends from Thursday to Saturday then Saturday to Monday. During these periods the management staff would only get about six hours sleep in total due to the intensity of the programme, but these weekends though exhausting, were great fun!

In the '80s, the gym equipment was rather sparse, purely a multi-gym located at the far end of the beauty corridor. Other than that there really was no gym equipment at all. A great deal of development had to take place before the Hall was in a position to provide a serious gym based workout for the dedicated guest. A slendertone room offered six couches on which the clients would relax while undergoing the electrically based treatment. This room had an inner room which held a Panthamol tank. Looking for all the world like a large blue coffin, the guest had to climb into it and be covered up to the neck. Then steam, Chime oils, and oxygen were pumped onto the skin, the treatment lasted for about an hour, but not surprisingly the treatment went out of fashion almost as soon as it came in. This end of the Hall boasted a sauna and a plunge pool which was not far above freezing temperature. This plunge pool really came into its own when staff members were leaving the Hall to move on to pastures new. At such times they were ceremoniously thrown into the pool, fully clothed, as part of the exit ritual. Eventually the pool was no longer required and as part of further development was demolished.

Keeping ahead of the times Ragdale Hall developed its own beauty school in the old stables. Riding no longer took place by now and all the horses had long since gone. Many of the Ragdale trained beauty therapists stayed on at Ragdale Hall for some of the developing years ahead This period of consolidation and reinforcement of high standards worked well for the business and in the marketplace, Ragdale's development had not gone unnoticed. The health hydro was a viable business now which in itself heralded the next change of ownership to a company called Theme Holdings.

Theme Holdings

Theme Holdings, an organization specialising in themed restaurants and venues, bought Ragdale Hall Health Hydro for £3.6 million – more than three times the 1984 price and marking up a considerable profit for Leisure Investments PLC who had originally purchased the business for £1 million.

Robert Upsdell accepted a position on the board of this new company. In this commercial development the Hall was transferred to a subsidiary company of Theme Holdings called Theme Holdings, Leisure Investments – Ragdale Hall Health Hydro. The organization continued under the day-to-day management of Martin Wooton.

For the next two years, refinement of the management systems continued, upgrading of all client information and staff incentive schemes were developed, together with the continued general updating and refurbishment of the Hall itself. During these years Jean Oliver held the position of Head of Beauty. Trevor Potter was the Chef, Vicky Hale virtually ran the Reception, Reservations, and Guest Liaison and David Sutton was now the Maintenance Manager. Martin Wooton had become involved in drawing up a business plan which centred on the Slimming Clubs, the Bath Spas and the idea of developing a holiday health hydro in Portugal. Through this initiative Theme Holdings – Leisure Investments approached Aspinals Leisure, owned by Peter De Savary, with whom they acquired a site on the eastern Algarve coast. The business plan being that the clientele could be brought from the high street into the slimming club, then into the health hydro in the UK and finally to the holiday hydro in the sun. It was at this point that a call from Robert Upsdell changed all the plans and the project was halted. He informed Martin that they were planning to sell the holding company and that he had to cease further project development at Ragdale Hall. After 10 years in post with Ragdale, Martin made a career move and went to work for Aspinals.

In 1989, as Martin Wooton left Ragdale Hall, Clare Brandish joined Leisure Developments (part of the Leisure Investments Group) as Hotel Manager, little knowing how involved and synonymous she was to become with the evolution of Ragdale Hall into the next millennium. What Clare found when she arrived at Ragdale Hall was an establishment out of step with the hotel industry she had just left. The Hall was just about to commence a £3 million extension and refurbishment programme. There was little or no importance attached to the hotel side of the business while there was a highly emphasised focus on the beauty side. The Hall was not computerised and the staff did not appear to be commercially aware. There were two entirely separate business sides running in parallel at the Hall, the hotel side and the beauty side and neither appeared to communicate with each other, making the possibility of mistakes rather high. Although in a failing market as the country slipped into recession Ragdale remained buoyed up by the high level of business that continued to be fed through to the Hall from the Slimming Clubs. "It was as if they still owned us," said Clare. Slimming Clubs were still using Ragdale Hall for much of their group leader events and rewards ceremonies, but these activities also petered out during the 1990s 5-year recession. Ragdale Hall was now having to seek new market sectors and respond to the new social demands from an ever more discerning clientele.

A programme of change was greatly needed to bring the business up to date and the hotel side of the Hall to a high standard within the industry. A wide remit of system changes, financial control and staff turnover had to be addressed in order to achieve a working concern that would survive in the aggressive commercial world of business. All this had to be achieved, whilst still retaining the retreat-like feel of this old country house.

Courtwell Group plc

In 1989 the Leisure Investment Group was a £98million concern. On December 1st 1989 the hosiery company Bearbrand Group put in a bid for the total Leisure Investment Group. As a result of this takeover, the enlarged group became known as Courtwell Group PLC. This commercial dinosaur was highly geared and proved too large and unwieldy to survive in the severe recessional market changes now emerging. It lasted just six months before it crashed.

During that six months Courtwell Group senior directors would arrive at the Hall in helicopters, looking rather severe and out of place, wearing their city suits during the brief visits they made. They remained remote from the staff and the day to day running of the Hall. Their attitude was somewhat instructional and directive and completely at odds with the environment that was Ragdale Hall. Staff did not understand this mentality and Clare found herself rallying them at this difficult time and trying to explain the rather distant approach the new owners were taking to the business. Suddenly the recession deepened and the economy spiralled downwards into what was to be the deepest and longest recession in British history. As a result the Courtwell Group PLC could not cope with this dynamic change and the group was plunged into the hands of the receivers. The future employment of the 150 staff working at Ragdale Hall suddenly looked precarious. Management held the operation together as best they could while they awaited news of their fate.

Cork Gulley were appointed on May 3rd 1990 as administrative receivers, on behalf of the group, to find a buyer for Ragdale Hall Health Hydro which was one of the few profitable parts of the ailing group of companies. At the time Ragdale's annual turnover had risen to £3million. Mr. Henry Nixon of Cork Gully received numerous enquires about the Hall and was confident that a buyer could be found, but he added, "it could take some time." The Ragdale Hall management team, led by Lesley White, decided to attempt a management buy out but the amount of money to be raised was considerable and, although they had some success in securing promise of several million pounds, they eventually reappraised their position and decided not to proceed with this move. During this period of uncertainty, several potential buyers viewed the Hall, the Purdew family from Henlow Grange, a venture capital company and the health insurance provider, BUPA, who wanted to turn the Hall into a rest home for the elderly. For various reasons they delayed their decision to buy. Then a couple of guys from the music industry showed up one day and snapped it up from under their noses.

Ragdale Hall (1990) Ltd.

In 1990 Garry Nesbitt and Michael Isaacs were looking around for another business to invest in following the sale of their company Our Price Records to W.H. Smith. Amazingly the opportunity to be informed about a new business prospect didn't come from an agent recruited for the job but a coincidental visit Garry made to his fitness club in Hampstead called The Ragdale Club. Together with the parent company, the club had suddenly gone into receivership and the manager of The Ragdale Club rushed over ashen faced, to speak to Garry and tell him the news. Garry called Michael and they contacted the receivers to arrange for the information to be sent to them. Initially the emphasis was on the London club itself until Garry's wife Penny, who had been to Ragdale Hall as a guest, suggested that they go and look at the Hall itself and experience the environment there.

The decision to buy the Hall was made quite quickly by Garry and Michael. They both say they will never forget the day they first arrived at the Hall. When they both walked through the front door they felt the place had a certain magic, "It had this amazing feel," said Garry. That instinctive first impression for these two entrepreneurs developed through to ownership in a very short time. Garry and Michael came along with a bankers draft for 4.6 million pounds, left it with the receiver and, without conditions, snapped up the health hydro business, Ragdale Hall. Some people would have said that this was a high price to pay and maybe they were right, considering the fact that the UK was moving into full-blown recession.

David Hamdorff of Levy Gee accountants in London had been drafted into the project to deliver profit forecasts on the potential of the business for Michael and Garry. The legal side of the deal was completed so fast it was possibly a record. Incredibly the legal conveyancing was worked out in an overnight session with their lawyers. The future of the Hall and the jobs of the employees that had looked so uncertain, was back on track in less than six weeks. For the first time since December 1959 the Hall, although still a commercial concern, commenced a period of private ownership. David Hamdorff decided to make a career move at this point and joined the newly formed Ragdale Hall (1990) Ltd as Financial Director.

Garry Nesbitt and Michael Isaacs, who were the founders of Our Price Records in December 1971, had entered into a business partnership again with the purchase of Ragdale Hall Health Hydro. However, following four owners in three years, the first approach of the new owners was to provide some stability and support. The in-house management team had done a terrific job of holding the operation together during this critical change period. As part of this stabilisation, Garry and Michael pledged to finish the 3 million pound extension and refurbishment programme already started by the previous owners. This meant that they had actually bought into the deal for £7.6million.

By this stage the country was going through a major transformation in expectation and quality of lifestyle. People were no longer prepared to allow the ageing process to develop unchecked as previous generations had done. There was a quest to stay healthier and younger looking into old age. Ragdale identified what market factors were changing and aligned itself with these changes to meet client demand - more so than at any time in its hydro history. The whole lifestyle awareness phase in society now took off and the "fat farm" image started to fade. From this point Ragdale Hall's image changed direction to remain in step with its clientele through the fast changing lifestyle whirlwind.

The next two years were a nightmare for the business. At the time of purchase the Hall was operational but an enormous excavation hole, with a few steel columns sticking out of the ground, existed at the side of the Hall together with an unsightly excavated area to the back of the building which had once been the rose garden. Works that had already started at the time of receivership were on hold, as several contractors had not received payment for the work already carried out and were understandably reluctant to continue the job. In fact contractors had rushed into the Hall when the news of receivership first broke, removing air conditioning equipment from the roof and radiators from the walls - much of which had just been installed the day before. All this happened in front of guests staying at the Hall and with a management team trying to maintain a sense of normality for both guests and staff. Unsure if they were risking further loss in continuing the work under the new ownership, the contractors needed balanced persuasion from the new management team to reduce panic and get the job restarted. Management at Ragdale explained as gently as they could that financial loss was inevitable unless they opted to finish the job. As a result the works were completed albeit slightly behind schedule but remarkably Ragdale Hall did not lose one contracting firm during the completion of this building project.

As soon as the Hall was purchased in June 1990 it was imperative that the building works be completed to the point where guests were able to stay in the Hall without too much disruption. This action, coupled with the cost of repairs and reinstating competitive pay scales, incurred large borrowing from Barclays Bank which plunged the business from a position of profit in 1989, the year before the new ownership, to a deficit of £700,000 in 1991.

The completion of the garden room and the commitment to finish a new block of eighteen superior bedrooms, commenced by the previous owners, placed a further drain on the coffers during what should have been a period of financial consolidation. It would have been tempting to convert these rooms into eighteen standard rooms, since the market for luxury health hydro accommodation had disappeared with the recession. However management were always convinced that the right path was to upgrade the facilities. Finally it took a complete closure of the Hall for two weeks in December 1990 to carry out final adjustment work, which completely rerouted the guest passageways through to the indoor pool and its new Jacuzzi. The indoor pool, opened only six years earlier, needed a completely new filtration system together with a full mechanical overhaul and this would have been impossible to carry out with guests in residence. Although Ragdale Hall reopened its doors just in time for Christmas 1990, the new wing of eighteen superior bedrooms didn't open until March 1991. Many inherited difficulties like this existed and so little time was available to make the right decisions for the future - yet the right decisions had to be made or the business would fail!

The initial management goals were to establish the operating systems and the accuracy of information and to get the Hall moving forward again in top gear as quickly as possible. Management took the decision to honour all guest commitments made by the old Ragdale Hall before the receivership. Gift vouchers for example, that had been sold to guests under the previous ownership, remained viable under the new ownership.

By 1991 the market was concentrating more on real value for money. The consumer had been taught a severe financial lesson during the recession. They no longer had that extra bit of disposable income that was common in the '80s. 1991 was a crunch year for the country in recession and it was no different for the health hydro industry. The disadvantage for Ragdale Hall was that it had been hit hard by the deep economic recession before it had had a chance to get back on its feet. Losses were being incurred by the beleaguered business due to the building works finishing under new ownership and, just to keep the Hall operating, essential replacement of worn out equipment was required by various departments. Borrowing facilities from Barclays Bank were almost spent. Trading was not good. Severe cut backs on costs wherever possible were absolutely essential for the continued existence of the business during this very difficult period. Rather than making wholesale redundancies the company was conscious to try and keep the team together. The complete company staff went from a five-day to a four-day working week to enable management to retain as much key skill as possible whilst still cutting costs. To facilitate their survival strategy in the failing market, the management team reduced their salaries by 20% for a few months.

*The Management
Team, 1991*

Everyone did his or her bit and everyone supported this approach. The loyalty shown by the staff was immense and their genuine concern for the company was overwhelming, but by the end of 1991 Ragdale was really feeling the severe effects of the deepening recession. Slimming Magazine, who had traditionally held a number of slimming events at Ragdale Hall throughout the '80s, ceased to do so as a direct result of the recessional economic environment.

Despite the seriousness of the situation management decided that they would go ahead with a company Christmas party. The staff had pulled together wonderfully and they deserved a night to relax and make merry. It was after the speeches at this party that Garry and Michael were to receive an unexpected show of loyalty from everyone. Julie Sim, who was PA to Garry and Michael at the time, mounted the stage to say a few words. She had one main message, that all the staff had a gift for Garry and Michael. Over the previous six months all staff had collected their tips and gratuities which would normally be shared out around the staff every three months and they wished this collection to be donated to the company to help towards the cost of the Christmas party. The total sum donated was £903.51. After all everyone had gone through this was an amazing gesture and a measure of the spirit that is still very much a part of Ragdale today. Garry and Michael were overwhelmed by this generosity but it left the directors in no doubt that their staff were behind them and wishing

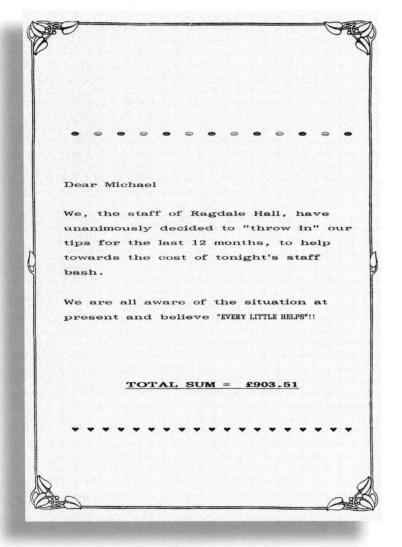

The certificate of donation for the Christmas party.

Dear Michael

We, the staff of Ragdale Hall, have unanimously decided to "throw in" our tips for the last 12 months, to help towards the cost of tonight's staff bash.

We are all aware of the situation at present and believe "EVERY LITTLE HELPS"!!

TOTAL SUM = £903.51

the company well. Ragdale Hall had a team of which few companies could boast. They were of one positive mind and that was to make it happen and make it happen now. How could they possibly fail?

Out in the market place liquidations were taking place everywhere and in every type of industry. To hold ground Ragdale Hall had to take a radical step or face the worst possible outcome. The order of the day was pure survival. The economy was in a very poor state. It took great courage, but the single most pivotal decision that management made was to reduce their prices in this severe recession. This was the big break through. Lowering the tariff prices enabled the guests, who were also feeling the pinch, to come to Ragdale Hall and get away from the madness. This action hoped to attract sufficient guests in high numbers to assist the Hall to cover overheads and purely remain operational with the aspiration that in time the economy would improve. In reality the result was so successful that the decision to lower tariff prices filled the Hall, kept the staff busy and reversed the loss of 1991 to a small profit in 1992. The business was again on its way. However it was to be a long recovery because it wasn't until 1997 that prices returned to where they were six years earlier in 1991.

"The company could have been compared to an oil tanker in that it took some considerable time to turn around after the rudder was full on," says David Hamdorff, now Managing Director, when describing the lengthy process they had faced. "Cashflow for the Hall was very tight for many years." By 1991 David began getting to grips with the business culture and the market forces that were putting a financial strain on the company. Marketing functions, which had been performed by outside consultants, were withdrawn from these agencies and the marketing department formed internally to drive the business promotion forward more cohesively. Modern hotel systems were established along with the installation of the first computer at Ragdale Hall to assist with client reservations.

Some staff structures were also changed during this time. Team dynamics had been causing concern as a considerable amount of demarcation existed throughout the departmental structure, which if left unaddressed, potentially, would have undermined the success of the business as a whole. Changes were sensitively explained and introduced to the teams commencing a period of attitude change and staff training that continues today. All departments were encouraged to realise that the overall success of the company depended on recognising the importance they played in the business as skilled teams. Housekeeping staff, who had laboured under low morale, developed a greater pride in their job and a sense of belonging. As with other departments, they came to understand the true value of their contribution to the company. Management took the opportunity of using this period of cash shortage to improve levels of customer care and the range of services available to guests. David Hamdorff revealed that "the lack of available funds almost forced us to focus on these areas, but this was a cathartic process and we worked incredibly hard on staff training". Consequently staff were looking and sounding more content than they had done for many years. Ragdale Hall was developing and its reputed friendly environment, under the ownership of Michael and Garry, was flourishing. People were beginning to like what they experienced at Ragdale. Guests started to return more frequently. As a result the Hall was just beginning to return to a reasonable profit margin and all staff were ready to provide the best service any guest had ever experienced.

During these years Garry and Michael reinvested all monies that the business made into the concern in order to support the rebuilding of the company. With their management team they always took the long-term view and in doing so assisted the upward curve of the company's recovery back to profitability as quickly as possible – a rare occurrence indeed in private business. This resulted in the company finances becoming healthier until in 1997 the last of the huge borrowed sum of £4.8million could be cleared. The turnaround strategy was so successful that it is not surprising that Ragdale Hall became a key client of Barclays Bank, who had remained supportive throughout. Since those days the company has always been very careful and considered in the changes they make. There have been slow and steady adjustments to staffing levels. Measured and much discussed price increases have allowed Ragdale to retain its middle of the road price band for clients. Initially there were very modest approaches to refurbishment to the fabric of the building. However in 1994 the Hall started the first of the refurbishment projects that, like the Forth Bridge, continues to the present time with the upgrading of bedrooms and theme designing of the public areas.

In 1995 the new pool complex was first discussed together with the other adventurous expansion programmes that are now available for the guest to both see and enjoy. With the benefit of hindsight it may have been possible to start these building projects as much as two years earlier, but it had been absolutely impossible to predict the speed of the market recovery and as so many had had their fingers burnt, no one was taking any chances.

In June 1995, Garry and Michael celebrated their fifth anniversary with Ragdale Hall. Clare Brandish had stepped into the role of Sales and Marketing Director for the enterprise and through her efforts and those of her team the market was opening up for Ragdale, developing an appeal which reached a wider group of people than ever before.

The health hydro guest of the '80s had metamorphosed along with the changes in the market. Now a variety of guests from different backgrounds and lifestyles visited the Hall. To implement all these changes and still retain the level of friendliness for which Ragdale is renowned was a tough challenge, but it was achieved. The success of the business depended on it. The Hall always had an excellent treatment reputation, built up from the Slimming Magazine days. However the beauty department has expanded from the seventeen beauty therapists originally employed by Tom Eyton. Today the department has grown to over one hundred beauty therapists and its reputation is now accepted as the best and the most extensive beauty department in the country.

The business is unique. Few organizations have such an intimate relationship with their clients but the natural warmth and professionalism of the beauty therapists make it all look and feel second nature. Slimming Magazine and Slimming Clubs are now two separate companies but in 1997 Clare Brandish re-established a link with Slimming Magazine who once again hold events at the Hall throughout the year.

By now the company had embarked on the most ambitious expansion programme in its history. The new breathtakingly designed spa complex boasting, an additional state of the art 25 metre swimming pool with water cascades, therapeutic massage jets and relaxation areas, was opened in October 1998.

Ragdale has developed an excellent reputation as a fitness centre, something that it could not boast in the early days. Starting with a multigym in the '80s at the far end of the beauty department, a lot of work had to be done to get a fitness centre underway that would be credible in the modern marketplace. Today the Hall has a fitness centre with a team that prides itself in providing a full workout service for guests whether they require a gentle exercise session or are taking a more robust approach. Expansion to the gym areas as well as the creation of two new studios was completed by August 1999.

The dining room that started off serving calorie controlled meals in the Slimming Magazine days, which the guests ate on old refectory tables, has developed beyond recognition into a sumptuous dining experience. Guests are served superb cuisine in a brand new, exquisite country house dining room retaining its homely, relaxed and cosy feel. The enlarged dining room, with its stunning stone-carved fireplace together with the new kitchens were completed by March 2000 and ceremonially opened by Pippa Woodroffe, niece of Philip Cantrell-Hubbersty, in April 2000. It was the first time that Pippa had returned to the hall since her Uncle Philip died in 1947. On the evening Pippa joined a special gathering of people, who represented almost one hundred years of Ragdale Hall ownership.

The final phase of this development was the opening of the "Verandah" wing and terrace in January 2001. Consisting of new refreshment area, further relaxation areas, lounges and additional superior style bedrooms. Ragdale Hall is now a truly modern establishment within the framework of an old country house. In order to maintain a top class service to a greater number of guests, Ragdale management has increased the team by a further one hundred staff.

At no time has management attempted to undermine the product they believe in, the health hydro business. In fact Garry and Michael personally test their own product on a regular basis keeping a finger on the pulse of the business and involving themselves in any changes that may be put forward as client requests. They did not try to take advantage of the new ownership situation to push prices up and drag in what monies they could in the difficult recessional situation. There were no sneaky hidden costs. The guests noticed all this and responded very favourably by dedicating their patronage to Ragdale Hall and its team. They came back for more and they continue to do so. Today Ragdale has a team of people who represent a complete transformation from the early days. Company demarcation lines have been dissolved, and teams and departments have been tightened and specialised to work cohesively with each other. Through experience a platform has been built, upon which the company of the future is being shaped.

Today everyone is welcome at Ragdale Hall whether they arrive in a helicopter, a Rolls Royce or on a bicycle. Everyone is equal here and everyone has the individual choice to make their stay what they want it to be. Unlike other health hydros, which boast of celebrities, Ragdale has its fair share of celebrities but believes that like everyone else, people in the public eye should be allowed to retain their anonymity. Today Ragdale offers a cocoon of sanctuary to all who wish to escape the pressures of their every day life. To assist this the guest will turn off their mobile phone. Their fax, computer and their daily timetable are all left in the world outside the main gate, allowing guests to really unwind and relax.

Having celebrated their 10th anniversary in the business, it is gratifying for Garry and Michael to look around and see many familiar faces of staff who have remained with them over the period of their ownership. Stability was brought to the Hall in the last decade and a future secured for all who wish to travel along the same road as

Ragdale. The staff numbers have grown from a team of one hundred and fifty in June 1990, to four hundred in January 2001 to meet the needs of its guests. The nature of the business dictates a high ratio of staff to guests. Today there is a ratio of more than two members of staff to every guest in the Hall. Ragdale likes to employ people who have a passion for the Hall and their job so that the guest continues to receive the best possible service and genuine concern.

There is always a need for organisations to continue self-examination to make sure mistakes are not made and to safeguard against becoming complacent with the comfortable status quo. Ragdale Hall is no exception in this. The Hall is currently one of the most significant employers in the Melton Mowbray area. As other large employers downsize their staff teams, Ragdale's increasing needs allow for the absorption of some of these skilled people reinforcing its position as a significant employer in the area. The majority of the people working at Ragdale come from the surrounding community and the Hall has benefited from their natural joie de vivre. When stressed guests arrive from other parts of the country or from major cities they are warmly greeted and made to feel most welcome by the natural friendliness of the staff. This friendly reputation has spread far and wide with guests often hearing of it before experiencing it for themselves. Like many other companies specialised staff are employed from all over the British Isles and the continent.

To assist clients to achieve easy access to existing and developing features of Ragdale Hall, the Hall has developed a comprehensive web site www.ragdalehall.co.uk which features a 3D plan of the ground floor of the Hall. Guests can view the new spa pool area, new dining room, or the new gymnasium and have a virtual tour of the facilities before committing to book. To get an idea of the beautiful countryside guests may visit, Ragdale has included a 180 degree sweep of the view from the balcony of the Terrace suite at the front of the house. On a good day the view can be clear for a stunning thirty miles.

The Local Community

The Hall enjoys its involvement with the local community. As in former times it plays an active part in the life of Ragdale Village. In the mid '90s the village wished to reopen their church, All Saints, following closure when the roof became unsafe, Ragdale Hall assisted the village with this reopening. This small community takes great pride in its village and in 1996 Ragdale Village was successful in achieving the "Best Kept Village Award" won in the hamlet section. Again in 1999 Ragdale Hall was instrumental in assisting the village to gain a new millennium bell for All Saints. Although the church, built of ironstone and mainly of 13th and 14th century had two ancient bells in the belfry, they had fallen silent for many years before Albert Cantrell-Hubbersty had built the bell tower at the new Ragdale Hall on the hill. Beams in the church belfry, supporting the bells had become unsafe and the bells could not be used. One of these bells, the oldest bell in Leicestershire dating back by its shape to circa 1300, is a 25.5 inch bell without an inscription. It had developed a 10inch crack in its soundbow which was first reported in 1876 by North when he wrote "The Church Bells of Leicestershire". The other ancient bell a Tenor measuring 27.5 inches is thought to possibly be a Johannes de Stafford bell dated circa 1350-1375. Its inscription reads "Ave Maria Gracia Plena Dns Tecum". The Parish Council were disappointed at the refusal of the Millennium Fund to assist with funding for part payment of their millennium bell and Ragdale Hall, who had already pledged a donation, stepped in to make up the short fall.

In May of 1999 the two ancient bells were lowered to the ground possibly for the first time in 700 years and taken to Taylors Bellfounders for repair. That summer the new millennium bell was cast by John Taylor and Co Loughborough in the presence of a large group of Ragdale Village parishioners and Róisín and Michael Isaacs of Ragdale Hall also attended this most important occasion. At the same time the Hall assisted in refurbishing the remaining timber works required in the belfry. All three bells were hung in the belfry fitted to a newly built timber frame for stationary chiming. They were dedicated on the 3rd of November 1999, just two months before the millennium was celebrated. The newest bell in Leicestershire, the millennium bell, is a treble, measuring 22.5 inches with an oak leaf ornament inscription band and Taylor badge which reads "Kindly donated by Ragdale Hall Health Hydro/September 1999" and opposite this "Ragdale's voice rings loud and clear once more".

The Hall is very proud of their involvement with the village and the new millennium bell for All Saints Church and wishes to continue its association with the village into the future. Along with this involvement the Hall assists with sponsorship of the Melton Mowbray Rugby Club, sponsorship of a young table tennis hopeful, James Milton, currently ranked number 5 in the British under 12's as well as sponsorship of Lara Crouch a young talented tennis player living in Ragdale Village.

Very much part of the Ragdale machinery is Pampurrs the cat. The incredible response to a competition to "Name that moggy" run in the Ragdale Hall Newsletter was quite overwhelming. Personal recollections of meeting the cat were recalled in graphic detail, how the cat reminded guests of their own cats both alive and deceased and the joy of having found a beautiful black cat at an establishment such as Ragdale. The Hall received imaginative offers of names such as Sitting Pretty, Lady Rags, Raggers, and Ragpuss. In the end the apt name of "Pampurrs" was chosen.

Garry and Michael still feel humbled by the fact that they own such a beautiful building. They admit that part of the success of the business has been because building extensions have been carried out with great sympathy for what was there in the beginning. All new building work has been in keeping with the original building style of Albert Cantrell-Hubbersty in 1908 to the point that it is difficult to tell the old from the new.

Today Ragdale Hall can enjoy the fruits of its success. The hard work and effort of yesteryear has paid off. The Hall received the accolade of being voted "Spa of the Year" by Professional Health and Beauty Magazine two years running in 1999 and again in 2000. The award, probably the most prestigious in the industry, is achieved only through nomination from clients. It is therefore with sheer delight that Ragdale received this recognition. By reputation Ragdale Hall is the market leader while on price it retains a middle of the road value for money position. Entry into this industry is prohibitive due to the initial cost. As a result there have been no new health hydros opened since the early '90s. This business is definitely a niche marketplace requiring specific skills and market knowledge much of which is gained through experience. Potential new entrants would have a difficult task with several sheer barriers to overcome. Market changes have been mostly along the development of hotels with conference facilities attached to a small spa containing a swimming pool, a small gym and a small number of beauty rooms. This type of market development does not impact negatively on the health hydro industry. In fact at this market level it is a positive development as it familiarises the general public with the concept of being pampered.

Since June 1990 the Hall has enjoyed its longest period of private ownership since the Cantrell-Hubbersty era. Garry and Michael have taken the house from the countryside and made it a household name throughout the nation. This could not have been achieved without a dedicated and caring team. Every team member from all departments has played their part in making Ragdale Hall the success it is today and every department is of equal significance in achieving the day to day running of the business. With Garry and Michael, their fellow Directors David Hamdorff and Clare Brandish, together with

Operations Managers Hugh Wilson, Emma Jane North, Allison Garner, Nicola Robson and Bob Rouse the house is now in safe and stable hands after forty years of precarious and uncertain ownership.

The challenge for the future is to continue to nurture the bussiness while retaining the feel of a country house. The secret is to keep the magic that is Ragdale Hall. Behind the scenes, there is always the need to recruit, train and retain the calibre of staff needed to maintain the standard that is Ragdale. People who will add to the continued development of the company over the years. While accepting this, Garry and Michael will ensure that the business does not lose its particular friendly, approachable culture. Influences for the future will continue to be driven by the needs of Ragdale's guests, particularly of relaxation. With an ever-higher profile in the marketplace Ragdale Hall looks forward to a bright future as a part of this absolutely amazing health hydro industry. From its cutting edge position, the company plans to remain instrumental in the development of this niche market sector.

The Parish of Ragdale, with its millennial heritage, remains one of the most beautiful and unspoilt parts of the country. The Hall which has withstood so much change over the centuries, continues to be a focal point in the community and the success of Ragdale Hall Health Hydro has ensured that visitors in previously unforeseen numbers, have enjoyed – and will continue to enjoy – this wonderful location in the heart of England.

Bibliography

Allen, Martin., (2000), *Hidden Agenda,* Macmillan Publishers Ltd, London.

Best, Geoffrey., (1985), *Mid-Victorian Britain,* Fontana Press, London.

Birkin, Henry, Sir ("Tim")., (1932), *The Full Throttle,* G.T. Foulis, & Co., Ltd, London.

Blow, Simon., (1983), *Fields Elysian,* J. M. Dent & Sons Ltd, London.

Blow, Simon., (1999), *No Time To Grow A Shattered Childhood,* John Murray (Publishers) Ltd, London.

Brownlow, Jack., *Melton Mowbray Queen Of The Shires,* Sycamore Press, Wymondham, Leicestershire.

Buxton, Meriel., (1987), *Ladies Of The Chase,* The Sportman's Press, London.

Clayton, Michael., (1987), *Prince Charles Horseman,* Stanley Paul, London.

Collinson, Hugh., (1981), *Rural Rides In Historic Leicestershire,* Peter Cooper Enterprises, Leicester.

De Courcy, Anne.,(2000), *The Viceroy's Daughters,* Weidenfeld & Nicolson, The Orion Publishing Group Ltd, London.

Dod's Parliamentary Companion Ltd., (1994), *The Prime Ministers,* The Creative Centre Limited, London.

Edwards, Lionel., (1991), *A Leicestershire Sketch Book,* The Haggerston Press, London.

Ellis, Colin. D. B., (1951), *Leicestershire And The Quorn Hunt,* Edgar Backus, Leicestershire.

Faber, Walter., (1932), *Wit And Wisdom,* Edgar Backus, Leicester.

Fox, James., (1998), *The Langhorne Sisters*, Granta Publications, London.

Godfrey, Rupert., (1998), *Letters From A Prince*, Little Brown & Company (UK), London.

Green, Johnnie., (1978), *Bentley Fifty Years Of The Marque*, Dalton Watson Ltd, London.

Hay, Michael., (1993), *Bentley Factory Cars 1919-1931*, Osprey, London.

Hickman, Trevor., (1998), *Melton Mowbray To Oakham*, Sutton Publishing Ltd, Stroud, Gloucestershire.

Itzkowitz, David. C., (1977), *Peculiar Privilege*, The Harvester Press Ltd, Sussex.

Leicestershire, Rutland Federation of Women's Institutes.,(1991), *The Leicestershire & Rutland Village Book*, MRM Associates Ltd, Reading.

Lovell, Mary. S., (1983), *A Hunting Pageant*, Saiga Publishing Co. Ltd., Surrey.

Newsome, David., (1998), *The Victorian World Picture*, Fontana press, Hammersmith, London.

Paget, Guy., (1936), *Bad Uns To Beat*, Collins Clear Type Press, London.

Paget, J, Otho., (1920), *Memories Of The Shires*, Methuen & Co. Ltd, London.

Pennell-Elmhirst, E, Captain., ("Brooksby"), (1883), *The Cream Of Leicestershire*, George Routledge, & Sons, London.

Powell, Bob., & Westcott, Nigel., (1997), *The Women's land Army 1939-1950*, Sutton Publishing Ltd, Gloucestershire.

Readers Digest., (1998), *Yesterday's Britain*, The Readers Digest Association Ltd, London.

Smith David J, (1989), *Britain's Military Airfields 1939-45*, Patrick Stephens Ltd, Wellingborough, Northamptonshire.

Stretton, John., (1997), *The Counties Of England Past & Present Leicestershire And Rutland* Past And Present Publishing Ltd, Peterborough.

Ziegler, Philip., (1990), *King Edward VIII*, William Collins & Co., London.

Index